THE PERFECT CRIME

RADICAL THINKERS

SET 1 ($12/£6/$14CAN)

MINIMA MORALIA
Reflections on a Damaged Life
THEODOR ADORNO
ISBN-13: 978 1 84467 051 2

FOR MARX
LOUIS ALTHUSSER
ISBN-13: 978 1 84467 052 9

THE SYSTEM OF OBJECTS
JEAN BAUDRILLARD
ISBN-13: 978 1 84467 053 6

LIBERALISM AND DEMOCRACY
NORBERTO BOBBIO
ISBN-13: 978 1 84467 062 8

THE POLITICS OF FRIENDSHIP
JACQUES DERRIDA
ISBN-13: 978 1 84467 054 3

THE FUNCTION OF CRITICISM
TERRY EAGLETON
ISBN-13: 978 1 84467 055 0

SIGNS TAKEN FOR WONDERS
On the Sociology of Literary Forms
FRANCO MORETTI
ISBN-13: 978 1 84467 056 7

THE RETURN OF THE POLITICAL
CHANTAL MOUFFE
ISBN-13: 978 1 84467 057 4

SEXUALITY IN THE FIELD OF VISION
JACQUELINE ROSE
ISBN-13: 978 1 84467 058 1

THE INFORMATION BOMB
PAUL VIRILIO
ISBN-13: 978 1 84467 059 8

CULTURE AND MATERIALISM
RAYMOND WILLIAMS
ISBN-13: 978 1 84467 060 4

THE METASTASES OF ENJOYMENT
On Women and Causality
SLAVOJ ŽIŽEK
ISBN-13: 978 1 84467 061 1

SET 2 ($12.95/£6.99/$17CAN)

AESTHETICS AND POLITICS
THEODOR ADORNO, WALTER BENJAMIN, ERNST BLOCH, BERTOLT BRECHT, GEORG LUKÁCS
ISBN-13: 978 1 84467 570 8

INFANCY AND HISTORY
On the Destruction of Experience
GIORGIO AGAMBEN
ISBN-13: 978 1 84467 571 5

POLITICS AND HISTORY
Montesquieu, Rousseau, Marx
LOUIS ALTHUSSER
ISBN-13: 978 1 84467 572 2

FRAGMENTS
JEAN BAUDRILLARD
ISBN-13: 978 1 84467 573 9

LOGICS OF DISINTEGRATION
Poststructuralist Thought and the Claims of Critical Theory
PETER DEWS
ISBN-13: 978 1 84467 574 6

LATE MARXISM
Adorno, Or, The Persistence of the Dialectic
FREDRIC JAMESON
ISBN-13: 978 1 84467 575 3

EMANCIPATION(S)
ERNESTO LACLAU
ISBN-13: 978 1 84467 576 0

THE POLITICAL DESCARTES
Reason, Ideology and the Bourgeois Project
ANTONIO NEGRI
ISBN-13: 978 1 84467 582 1

ON THE SHORES OF POLITICS
JACQUES RANCIÈRE
ISBN-13: 978 1 84467 577 7

STRATEGY OF DECEPTION
PAUL VIRILIO
ISBN-13: 978 1 84467 578 4

POLITICS OF MODERNISM
Against the New Conformists
RAYMOND WILLIAMS
ISBN-13: 978 1 84467 580 7

THE INDIVISIBLE REMAINDER
On Schelling and Related Matters
SLAVOJ ŽIŽEK
ISBN-13: 978 1 84467 581 4

THE PERFECT CRIME

Jean Baudrillard

Translated by Chris Turner

VERSO

London • New York

Published with the financial assistance of the French Ministry of Culture

First published by Verso 1996
This edition published by Verso 2008
Copyright © Verso 2008
Translation © Chris Turner 1996
First published as *Le crime parfait* by Editions Galilée 1995
Copyright © Editions Galilée 1995
All rights reserved

3 5 7 9 10 8 6 4 2

Verso
UK: 6 Meard Street, London W1F 0EG
USA: 180 Varick Street, New York, NY 10014-4606
www.versobooks.com

Verso is the imprint of New Left Books

ISBN-13: 978-1-84467-203-5

British Library Cataloguing in Publication Data
A catalogue record for this book is available from the British Library

Library of Congress Cataloging-in-Publication Data
A catalog record for this book is available from the Library of Congress

Typeset by Hewer Text UK Ltd, Edinburgh
Printed by ScandBook AB, Sweden

'So, my friend, after the example of the Phoenicians, you charted your course by the stars?'

'No,' said Menippus, 'it was among the stars themselves I journeyed.'

Given the mass of evidence, there is no plausible hypothesis but reality.
Given the mass of evidence to the contrary, there is no solution but illusion.

Contents

TRANSLATOR'S ACKNOWLEDGEMENTS

I would like to thank Marie-Dominique Maison, Leslie Hill, Glynis Powell, Mike Gane, Yasmina Lallemand and the author for their help, both direct and indirect, with parts of this translation. As ever, of course, I take sole responsibility for its shortcomings. All the notes are my own.

This is the story of a crime – of the murder of reality. And the extermination of an illusion – the vital illusion, the radical illusion of the world. The real does not disappear into illusion; it is illusion that disappears into integral reality.

If the crime were perfect, this book would have to be perfect too, since it claims to be the reconstruction of the crime.

Alas, the crime is never perfect. Moreover, in this grim record of the disappearance of the real, it has not been possible to pin down either the motives or the perpetrators, and the corpse of the real itself has never been found.

And the idea which underlies the book has never been pinned down either. That idea was the murder weapon.

Though the crime is never perfect, perfection, true to its name, is always criminal. In the perfect crime it is the perfection itself which is the crime, just as, in the transparence of evil,[1] it is the transparence itself that is the evil. But perfection is always punished: the punishment for perfection is reproduction.

Are there extenuating circumstances to this crime? Certainly not, since these always have to be sought among the motives or the perpetrators. But the crime has no motivation and no perpetrator, and therefore remains perfectly inexplicable. This is its true perfection. Though admittedly, from the point of view of the concept, this is more of an aggravating circumstance.

Though the consequences of the crime are never-ending, there is neither murderer nor victim. If there were either, the secret of the crime would be unmasked some day, and the inquiry concluded. The secret, in the end, is that the two are merged: 'In the last analysis, the victim and the persecutor are one. We can only grasp the unity of the human race if we can grasp, in all its horror, the truth of this ultimate equivalence' (Eric Gans).

In the last analysis, object and subject are one. We can only grasp the essence of the world if we can grasp, in all its irony, the truth of this radical equivalence.

The Perfect Crime

Were it not for appearances, the world would be a perfect crime, that is, a crime without a criminal, without a victim and without a motive. And the truth would forever have withdrawn from it and its secret would never be revealed, for want of any clues [*traces*] being left behind.

But the fact is that the crime is never perfect, for the world betrays itself by appearances, which are the clues to its non-existence, the traces of the continuity of the nothing. For the nothing itself – the continuity of the nothing – leaves traces. And that is the way the world betrays its secret. That is the way it allows itself to be sensed, while at the same time hiding away behind appearances.

The artist, too, is always close to committing the perfect crime: saying nothing. But he turns away from it, and his work is the trace of that criminal imperfection. The artist is, in Michaux's words, the one who, with all his might, resists the fundamental drive not to leave traces.[2]

The perfection of the crime lies in the fact that it has always-already been accomplished – *perfectum*. A misappropriation of the world as it is, before it even shows itself. It will never, therefore, be discovered. There will be no Last Judgement to punish or pardon it. There will be no end, because things have always-already happened. Neither resolution nor absolution, but inevitable unfolding of the consequences. Precession of the original crime – which we might perhaps be said to find in derisory form in the current precession of simulacra. After that, our destiny is the accomplishment of this crime, its inexorable unfolding, the continuity of the evil, the continuation of the nothing. We shall never experience the primal scene, but at every moment we experience its prolongation and its expiation. There is no end to this and the consequences are incalculable.

Just as we cannot plumb the first few seconds of the Big Bang, so we cannot locate those few seconds in which the original crime took place either. It is a fossilized crime, then, like the 'fossilized' background noise scattered about the universe. And it is the energy of that crime, like that of the initial explosion, which will spread through the world until, perhaps, it exhausts itself.

This is the mythic vision of the original crime, the vision of the alter-ation[3] of the world in the play of seduction and appearances, and of its definitive illusoriness.

This is the form the mystery takes.

The great philosophical question used to be 'Why is there something rather than nothing?' Today, the real question is: 'Why is there nothing rather than something?'

The absence of things from themselves, the fact that they do not take place though they appear to do so, the fact that everything withdraws behind its own appearance and is, therefore, never identical with itself, is the material illusion of the world. And, deep down, this remains the great riddle, the enigma which fills us with dread and from which we protect ourselves with the formal illusion of truth.

On pain of dread, we have to decipher the world and therefore wipe out the initial illusoriness of the world. We can bear neither the void, nor the secret, nor pure appearance. And why should we decipher it instead of letting its illusion shine out as such, in all its glory? Well, the fact that we cannot bear its enigmatic character is also an enigma, also part of the enigma. It is part of the world that we cannot bear either the illusion of the world or pure appearance. We would be no better at coping with radical truth and transparency, if these existed.

Truth wants to give herself naked. She is desperately seeking nudity, like Madonna in the film which brought her fame. That hopeless striptease is the very striptease of reality, which 'disrobes' in the literal sense,[4] offering up to the eyes of gullible voyeurs the appearance of nudity. But the fact is that this nudity wraps it in a second skin, which no longer has even the erotic charm of the dress. There is no longer any need even of bachelors to strip her bare, since she has herself given up *trompe-l'œil* for striptease.

And, indeed, the main objection to reality is its propensity to submit unconditionally to every hypothesis you can make about it. With this its most abject conformism, it discourages the liveliest minds. You can subject it – and its principle (what do they get up to together, by the way, apart from dully copulating and begetting reams of obviousness?) – to the most cruel torments, the most obscene provocations, the most paradoxical insinuations. It submits to everything with unrelenting servility. Reality is a bitch. And that is hardly surprising, since it is the product of stupidity's fornication with the spirit of calculation – the dregs of the sacred illusion offered up to the jackals of science.

To recover the trace of the nothing, of the incompleteness, the imperfection of the crime, we have, then, to take something away from the reality of the world. To recover the constellation of the mystery [*secret*],[5] we have to take something away from the accumulation of reality and language. We have to take words from language one by one, take things from reality one by one, wrest the same away from the same. Behind every fragment of reality, something has to have disappeared in order to ensure the continuity of the nothing – without, however, yielding to the temptation of annihilation, for disappearance has to remain a living disappearance, and the trace of the crime a living trace.

What we have forgotten in modernity, by dint of constantly accumulating, adding, going for more, is that force comes from subtraction, power from absence. Because we are no longer capable today of coping with the symbolic mastery of absence, we are immersed in the opposite illusion, the disenchanted illusion of the proliferation of screens and images.

Now, the image can no longer imagine the real, because it is the real. It can no longer dream it, since it is its virtual reality. It is as though things had swallowed their own mirrors and had become transparent to themselves, entirely present to themselves in a ruthless transcription, full in the light and in real time. Instead of being absent from themselves in illusion, they are forced to register on thousands of screens, off whose horizons not only the real has disappeared, but the image too. The reality has been driven out of reality. Only technology perhaps still binds together the scattered fragments of the real. But what has become of the constellation of meaning in all this?

The only suspense which remains is that of knowing how far the world can derealize itself before succumbing to its reality deficit or, conversely, how far it can hyperrealize itself before succumbing to an excess of reality (the point when, having become perfectly real, truer than true, it will fall into the clutches of total simulation).

Yet it is not certain that the constellation of the mystery is wiped out by the transparency of the virtual universe, nor that the power of illusion is swept away by the technical operation of the world. Behind all technologies one can sense a kind of absolute affectation and double game, their very exorbitance turning them into a game by which the world shows through, from behind the illusion of its being transformed. Is technology the lethal alternative to the illusion of the world, or is it merely a gigantic avatar of the same basic illusion, its subtle final twist, the last hypostasis?

Perhaps, through technology, the world is toying with us, the object is seducing us by giving us the illusion of power over it. A dizzying hypothesis: rationality, culminating in technical virtuality, might be the last of the ruses of unreason, of that will to illusion of which, as Nietzsche says, the will to truth is merely a derivative and an avatar.

On the horizon of simulation, not only has the world disappeared but the very question of its existence can no longer be posed. But this is perhaps a ruse of the world itself. The iconolaters of Byzantium were subtle folk, who claimed to represent God to his greater glory but who, simulating God in images, thereby dissimulated the problem of his existence. Behind each of these images, in fact, God had disappeared. He was not dead; he had disappeared. That is to say, the problem no longer even arose. It was resolved by simulation. This is what we do with the problem of the truth or reality of this world: we have resolved it by technical simulation, and by creating a profusion of images in which there is nothing to see.

But is it not the strategy of God himself to use images in order to disappear, himself obeying the urge to leave no trace?

So the prophecy has been fulfilled: we live in a world where the highest function of the sign is to make reality disappear and, at the same time, to mask that disappearance. Art today does the same. The media today do the same. That is why they are doomed to the same fate.

Because nothing wants exactly to be looked at any longer, but merely to be visually absorbed and circulate without leaving a trace – thus outlining, as it were, the simplified aesthetic form of impossible exchange – it is difficult today to recover a grasp on appearances. With the result that the discourse which would account for them would be a discourse in which there was nothing to say – the equivalent of a world where there is nothing to see. The equivalent of a pure object, of an object which is not an object. The harmonious equivalence of nothing to nothing, of Evil to Evil. But the object which is not an object continues to obsess you by its empty, immaterial presence. The whole problem is: on the outer fringes of the nothing, to materialize that nothing; on the outer fringes of the void, to trace out the mark of the void; on the outer fringes of indifference, to play by the mysterious rules of indifference.

There is no point identifying the world. Things have to be grasped in their sleep, or in any other circumstance where they are absent from themselves. As in the *House of the Sleeping Beauties*,[6] where the old men spend the night beside the women and, though mad with desire, do not touch them, and slip away before they wake. They too are lying next to an object which is not an object, the total indifference of which heightens the erotic charge. But the most enigmatic thing is that it is not possible to know whether the women are really asleep or whether they are not maliciously taking pleasure, from the depths of their sleep, in their seductiveness and their own suspended desire.

Not to be sensitive to this degree of unreality and play, this degree of malice and ironic wit on the part of language and the world is, in effect, to be incapable of living. Intelligence is precisely this sensing of the universal illusion, even in amorous passion – though without the natural course of that passion being impaired. There is something stronger than passion: illusion. There is something stronger than sex or happiness: the passion for illusion.

There is no point identifying the world. We cannot even identify our own faces, since mirrors impair their symmetry. To see our own face as it is would be madness, since we would no longer have any mystery for ourselves and would, therefore, be annihilated by transparency. Might it not be said that man has evolved into a form such that his face remains invisible to him and he becomes definitively unidentifiable, not only in the mystery of his face, but in any of his desires? But it is the same with any object which reaches us only in a definitively alter-ed state, even when it does so on the screen of science, in the mirrors of information or on the screens of our brains. Thus, all things offer themselves up without a hope of being anything other than illusions of themselves. And it is right that this should be so.

Fortunately, the objects which appear to us have always-already disappeared. Fortunately, nothing appears to us in real time, any more than do the stars in the night sky. If the speed of light were infinite, all the stars would be there simultaneously and the celestial vault would be an unbearable incandescence. Fortunately, nothing takes place in real time. Otherwise, we would be subjected, where information is concerned, to the light of all events, and the present would be an unbearable incandescence. Fortunately, we live on the basis of a vital illusion, on the basis of an absence, an unreality, a non-immediacy of things. Fortunately, nothing is instantaneous, simultaneous or contemporary. Fortunately, nothing is present or identical to itself. Fortunately, reality does not take place. Fortunately, the crime is never perfect.

"Daniel's Paragraph"

The Spectre of the Will

The radical illusion is that of the original crime, by which the world is alter-ed from the beginning, and is never identical to itself, never real. The world exists only through this definitive illusion which is that of the play of appearances – the very site of the unceasing disappearance of all meaning and all finality. And this is not merely metaphysical: in the physical order, too, from its origin – whatever that may be – the world has been forever appearing and disappearing.

An alter-ation which tends to diminish with increasing information and which will, in the end, be eliminated by absolute information: the world's equivalence to the world – the final illusion, that of a world which is perfect, fully realized, fully effectuated, a world which is consummated and has attained the height of existence and reality, and also the furthermost extent of its possibilities. It is God (this we cannot hide) who stands at the end of this process of increasing information and complex-ification, of verification of the world in real time. It is God who presides over this dissolution of the world as illusion and its resurrection as simulacrum and virtual reality, at the end of a process of extenuation of all its possibilities by the real. It is God who presides over the unconditional realization of the world and its final illusion. God is never at the origin, but always at the end. And so we can say that that end is necessarily an unhappy one, and it is as well to leave it hanging.[7]

The fact that the world is illusion follows from its radical imperfection. If everything had been perfect, the world would quite simply not exist and if, by some misfortune, it were to become so again, it would quite simply not exist any more. This is the essence of crime: if it is perfect, it leaves no clue, no trace. So what guarantees the world's existence for us is its accidental, criminal, imperfect character. And it follows from this that it can be given to us only as illusion.

All that is projected beyond this illusion, beyond this accidental manifestness of the world, which forever distances it from its meaning and origin, is merely a justificatory phantasy. The projecting back of a phantom causality and intelligibility, of an exceptional order which merely confirms the rule of accidental disorder and is, doubtless, merely one episode in that disorder.

We oscillate between an illusion and a truth which are each equally unbearable. But perhaps truth is even more unbearable, and we ultimately desire the illusion of the world, even if we take up all the arms of truth, science and metaphysics against it. Our latent truth is that of nihilism, but, as Nietzsche writes, 'truth cannot be regarded as the highest power. The will to semblance, to illusion, to deception, to becoming, to change (to objective deception) is to be regarded here as deeper, more original, more metaphysical than the will to truth, to reality, to being – the latter is itself merely a form of the will to illusion.'

['*Aber die Wahrheit gilt nicht als oberste Macht. Der Wille zum Schein, zur Illusion, zur Täuschung, zum Werden, zum Wechseln (zur objektiven Täuschung) gilt hier als tiefer, ursprünglicher, metaphysischer als der Wille zur Wahrheit, zur Wirklichkeit, zum Sein – letzterer ist selbst bloss eine Form des Willens zur Illusion.*']

How can we believe in the truth of what has neither principle nor end? All we can add to it is this little final illusion, together with the causal illusion of a non-accidental effect – a reparative illusion when set against the devastating illusion of the world. But this is merely an artificial supplement. Our consciousness, by which we aspire to outdo the world, is merely a secondary excess, the phantom extremity of a world for which this simulation of consciousness is entirely superfluous. We shall never achieve anything equivalent, by act of will, to the accidental irruption of the world.

We cannot project more order or disorder into the world than there is. We cannot transform it more than it transforms itself. This is the weakness of our historical radicality. All the philosophies of change, the revolutionary, nihilistic, futurist utopias, all this poetics of subversion and transgression so characteristic of modernity, will appear naive when compared with the instability and natural reversibility of the world. Not only transgression, but even destruction is beyond our reach. We shall never, by an act of destruction, achieve the equivalent of the world's accidental destruction.

What we can add by artificial destruction already falls within the scope of the world's own ceaseless revolution, the ironic trajectory of particles and the chaotic turbulence of natural systems. And the final accident is no more within our power than the initial accident. Here, once again, we must not delude ourselves. We shall add nothing to the nothingness of the world, since we are part of it. But we shall add nothing to its meaning either, since it does not have any.

Excess is the world's excess, not ours. It is the world that is excessive, the world that is sovereign.

This protects us from the illusion of the will, which is also that of faith and desire. The metaphysical illusion of having some effect and frustrating the continuation of the nothing.

Our will is like a phantom pregnancy or an artificially innervated prosthesis. Or the 'virtual' suffering of the phantom limb that follows the amputation of the real one (all virtual reality is the product, like this, of a surgical operation on the real world). The will is of this same order. Its extrapolation into the affairs of the world is merely the extrapolation of desire, or of the suffering of the phantom limb. Dreams, too, give us the illusion that we are in control of them, or can delay their coming to their term. They even give us the illusion of being aware of dreaming, which is part of their mechanism. This is the clinamen of the will interfering with the chromosomes of the dream.

As in dreams, the will must espouse this accidental declension of the world – must inflect, not reflect (on), itself. Must be merely itself an unexpected continuation which perpetuates the event of the world, and perhaps hastens it on its course. Must be in no way different from desire.

In Nabokov, in the gracious universe of *Ada*, as in the tragic universe, there are never any decisions. Everything is made up of – happy or unhappy – accidents. There is neither misdeed nor remorse. Everything is immoral and, as a result, so sensual. Not just bodies, but the will itself becomes sensual and accidental. The actors do not believe in their own existence, and do not take responsibility for it. They are happy just to obey the successive promptings of their will and their desire, to respect the enigmatic incidence of these things, while observing certain rules of the game towards existence, the first of which is not to consent to it.

Existence is something we must not consent to. It has been given to us as a consolation prize, and we must not believe in it. The will is something we must not consent to. It has been given to us as the illusion of an autonomous subject. Now, if there is anything worse than being subject to the law of others, it is surely being subject to one's own law. The real is something we must not consent to. It has been given to us as simulacrum, and the worst thing is to believe in it for want of anything else. The only thing we should consent to is the rule. But in that case, we are speaking not of the rule of the subject, but the rule of the way of the world [*jeu du monde*].

The real, for its part, is merely the natural child of disillusion. Which is itself a secondary illusion. Faith in reality is, of all the imaginary forms, the basest and most trivial.

Yet determination is extending its grasp, and the field of what is now ours to decide is expanding daily. We are no longer free not to will. We have to will even where we have no wish to.

And why stop there? We shouldn't just consult the parents on the choice of sex, but the embryos themselves. Then, at least, the absurdity of the situation would be plain for all to see. The fact is that we are, most often, in a situation of having to decide on matters we know nothing of and have no wish to know anything of. The power of others to have control of one's life is an abuse. But each person's right and duty to have control of him- or herself is even more dangerous. This is how voluntary servitude has transformed itself into its opposite – being commanded to desire, commanded to exercise freedom and choice – which is the consummate form of that servitude. The will is entrapped by the limitless freedom it is accorded, and consents to this out of an illusion of self-determination.

Now, the same order reigns over wills as reigns in biology. The same random and automatic regulation applies to wills in our operational universe as applies in the distribution of sexes at birth or in the freely expressed opinions of millions of citizens, which produces the same statistical outcome as would be achieved by consulting monkeys.

Where, then, does this wish to substitute the human will for the random course of things come from? There remains, of course, the glory of artifice and of frustrating the natural order. We want to will – that is the secret – just as we want to believe and want to be able [*pouvoir*], because the idea of a world without will, belief and power [*pouvoir*] is unbearable to us. But most of the time we can will only what has already come to fruition. So the Student of Prague arrives on the duelling ground and his opponent is already dead – his double has passed that way.[8] Precession of the double, of the involuntary operator of desire. Precession of the event, of the effect over the cause – metalepsis of the will.

The anteriority of the will is always stressed, as is the cause's preceding of the effect. But most often, the will merges with the event as its retrospective *mise en scène*, in the same way as a dream sequence gives expression to the physical sensation of the sleeping body. In any case, whatever one wills, subsequent events will still be of the order of the fateful – that is, of what happens to you, for good or ill, inadvertently – though not without some secret connection between them.

Why, then, should we will? Why should we desire? We cannot do otherwise. We have to contribute by our desires or our wills to the coming to term of a world in which they have no part. This is our involuntary contribution to our own destinies. According to Nietzsche, this drive is so great in man that for fear of desiring nothing, he will prefer the desire for the nothing, thus making himself, by the deployment of a will without object, the surest agent of that continuity of the nothing which is the continuation of the original crime.

'Why is there nothing rather than something?' There is, ultimately, no answer to this, since the nothing originates in myth, in the original crime, whereas the something originates in what, by convention, we call reality. Now, the real is never sure. The question then becomes, not 'Where does illusion come from?', but 'Where does the real come from?' How is it that there even is a reality effect? That is the true enigma. If the world was real, how is it that it did not become rational long ago? If it is merely illusion, how can a discourse of reality and the rational even arise? But that is the question. Is there anything but a *discourse* of the real and the rational? Perhaps there never has been any kind of progress towards more science, consciousness and objectivity, and all this has merely been talk on the part of intellectuals and ideologues who, for three centuries, have derived considerable advantage from it.

The same problem arises in the physical sciences. Bruno Jarrosson writes:

The first reaction of the fathers of quantum physics at the aberrations coming out of their equations (collapse of the universe of reference: time, space, the principle of identity and of the excluded middle, inseparability, non-locality of particles) was to regard the microscopic world as radically strange and mysterious. Such an interpretation is not, however, the most logical. For the microscopic world is to be accepted as it is. If we cannot derive a conception of the macroscopic world from it, then the mystery lies in the macroscopic world. From that point, we have to think that the strangest thing is not the strangeness of the microscopic world, but the non-strangeness of the macroscopic. Why are the concepts of identity, excluded middle, time and space operative in the macroscopic world? That is what we have to explain. (*Du micro au macro – le mystère des évidences*)

Since the universe of reference has become unintelligible, reason, being part of that universe, cannot but pose the question of its own existence: how can measurable time exist, how can elements and bodies exist separately? Given the uncertainty principle, how can there be an object and a subject of science?

Similarly, the real, having become unintelligible, poses an insoluble question for reason, which is part of it: How is it that the concepts of reality, objectivity, truth, causality and identity can function? Why does something seem to exist rather than nothing?

But in fact there is nothing.

Why is there will rather than no will?

But there is no will. There is no real. There isn't something. There is nothing. Or, in other words, the perpetual illusion of an ungraspable object and the subject who believes he grasps it. The illusion of a Thing and a rational causality which is, admittedly, comforting to our intellects, but unimaginable in any other universe, including that of particle physics. As Updike says, God is solely responsible for what we can see and hear, but in no way for anything whatever at the microscopic level.

So no purpose is served by attempting to reconcile the order of the will with that of the world to the philosophical advantage of the latter. There is the continuity of the world, as it has meaning for us, and the continuity of the world as, in secret, it is nothing and means nothing. This latter does not, strictly speaking, exist. It cannot be verified, but can only betray itself, only 'show through' [*transparaître*] like evil, squint out through appearances. There is no dialectic between the two orders. Each is alien to the other.

The Radical Illusion

So the world, then, is a radical illusion. That is, at least, one hypothesis. At all events, it is an unbearable one. And to keep it at bay, we have to realize the world, give it force of reality, make it exist and signify at all costs, take from it its secret, arbitrary, accidental character, rid it of appearances and extract its meaning, divert it from all predestination and restore it to its end and its maximum efficacy, wrest it from its form to deliver it up to its formula. This gigantic enterprise of disillusionment – of, literally, putting the illusion of the world to death, to leave an absolutely real world in its stead – is what is properly meant by simulation.

It is not, then, the real which is the opposite of simulation – the real is merely a particular case of that simulation – but illusion. And there is no crisis of reality. Far from it. There will always be more reality, because it is produced and reproduced by simulation, and is itself merely a model of simulation. The proliferation of reality, its spreading like an animal species whose natural predators have been eliminated, is our true catastrophe. This is the inevitable fate of an objective world.

We have to restore the potency and the radical meaning of illusion, which is most often reduced to the level of a chimaera diverting us from what is true: what things deck themselves out in to hide what they are. When, in fact, the illusion of the world is the way things have of presenting themselves for what they are when they are not actually there at all. In appearance, things are what they give themselves out to be. They appear and disappear without letting anything at all show through. They unfurl without concern for their being, or even for their existence. They signal to us, but are not susceptible of decipherment. On the other hand, in simulation, in this giant *dispositif* of meaning, calculation and efficiency that encompasses all our technical devices, including current virtual reality, the illusion of the sign is lost, and only its operation remains. The happy non-distinction between true and false, between real and unreal, gives way to the simulacrum, which consecrates the unhappy non-distinction between true and false, between the real and its signs, the unhappy, necessarily unhappy, destiny of meaning in our culture.

We continue to manufacture meaning, even though we know there is none. It remains to be seen, in fact, whether the illusion of meaning is a vital illusion or one that is destructive of the world and the subject itself. However this may be, faced with this strategy on the part of the subject, the world develops a much more subtle and paradoxical one, which is to give itself out for what it is, when it is actually not there. Over against the subject, that indomitable producer of meaning, stands the world, that inexhaustible producer of illusion, including, no doubt – with the involuntary complicity of the subject – the illusion of meaning.

There will be no end to this frenzied race around the Möbius strip where the surface of meaning perpetually feeds into the surface of illusion, unless the illusion of meaning were to win out once and for all, which would put an end to the world.

The whole of our history bears witness to this machinery of reason, which is itself now coming apart. Our culture of meaning is collapsing beneath the excess of meaning, the culture of reality collapsing beneath the excess of reality, the information culture collapsing beneath the excess of information – the sign and reality sharing a single shroud.

They are trying to persuade us that technology will inevitably produce good, to give a role to the artificial environment as a second nature, to select only automatic reflexes in line with a kind of mental genetic code. They are trying to wipe out all the supernatural reflexes of thought, of that thought which reacts instinctively to the illusion of the world, turns appearances back on reality, uses the illusion of the world against the world itself: the Manichaean understanding of evil, the understanding of the world as machination. It is said that the state of nature is unthinkable, because in that state thought does not exist. But this is exactly what we are moving towards: a state of pure operational intelligence, and thus of radical disillusioning of thought.

This dream of extirpating all the magic from thought, of eliminating every principle of evil, is as absurd as the dream of eliminating all concupiscence, even in dreams.

If the heresy of appearances is our original crime, then every rational impulse to eliminate it is the symptom of a fantastic error on the part of the will, the symptom of an aberration of desire.

At all events, illusion is indestructible. The world as it is – which is not at all the 'real' world – perpetually eludes the investigation of meaning, thus causing the present catastrophe of the apparatus of production of the 'real' world, so true is it that illusion cannot be combated with truth – that is merely to redouble the illusion – but only by a higher illusion.

The only response to the phantasmagoria of worlds-beyond, the latest and most subtle of which is the artificial synthesis of this world, is the higher illusion of our world.

Every revolution brings about a general involution in a kind of downward spiral. This negative spiral can be countered only by striking an opposite blow, by upping the stakes – outdoing insignificance with the nothing, the visible with appearance, the false with illusion, evil with greater evil.

The radical illusion of the world cannot be dispelled. The illusion of dispelling it is the secondary illusion of the disavowal and transformation of the world. But perhaps, in going to its extreme, that movement gets caught up in its own game and ends up wiping out its own traces, leaving the field free for misappropriation, imperfection, the original crime? Perhaps there is a ruse of the world, just as there is a ruse of history, and rationality and perfection in general might merely be implementing its irrational decree? Sciences and technologies would then merely be an immense, ironic diversion on the horizon of its disappearance.

What within truth is merely truth falls foul of illusion. What within truth exceeds truth is of the order of a higher illusion. Only what exceeds reality can go beyond the illusion of reality.

Trompe-l'œil Genesis

Bertrand Russell's paradox in *The Analysis of Mind*, in which the world is supposed to have been created only a few minutes ago but peopled with a humanity which remembers an illusory past, is well-known.

We might, in this connection, revive the hypothesis of P.H. Gosse, the nineteenth-century English naturalist, in his book *Omphalos* (which Stephen J. Gould discusses in *The Flamingo's Smile*), that all the geological and fossil traces of the origin and evolution of species, including the human species, are a simulation contemporaneous with the creation of the world by God five thousand years ago, as in the biblical account.

Everything which appears to reach back beyond that point, right down into the depths of time, has, he alleges, merely been got up by God in his infinite kindness to bestow an origin and a history upon our world, and is intended to create the illusion of elapsed time. God, argues Gosse, gave men a past in order to soften the unbearable confrontation with the world as it is, the product of an act of force on the part of a higher will. We can no longer even imagine the brutality of the creative act, but God has perhaps taken this into account and, in compensation, provided us with a simulacrum of history, to make man's existence bearable to him. Obviously, we can ask: did God really take pity on the human race, or is this merely a gratuitous joke, to mock man once again by holding out before him the forbidden fruit of the knowledge of his own origins, whereas this is in fact merely a mirage?

Gosse's suggestion is, at all events, extraordinary: to safeguard biblical revelation, he makes God an evil genius of simulation. Is there not a subtle impiety in this? God might have contented himself with creating the world, without inventing this *trompe-l'œil* anamorphosis. So that could only have been the product of his malicious pleasure. This immediately makes him quite a like-able character, even if it does so to future archaeologists' cost, doomed as they will be to live in permanent uncertainty. For Gosse argues: 'as thoughts in God's mind, solidified in stone by creation *ab nihilo*, strata and fossils are just as true as if they recorded the products of conventional time'.[9] If the unreal past is no less true than our objective reality, then this latter is no more true than that unreal past. And we can say, with the Ecclesiast, 'The simulacrum is not what conceals the truth, it is the truth which conceals that there is none. The simulacrum is true.'[10]

Fortunately, all this is false, dictated by a blind and illogical faith. Yet if we take away the prejudice of faith, and retain only the simulation hypothesis, Gosse's idea opens on to some surprising horizons and one quite serious possibility. It even assumes a prophetic air. For his hypothesis is indeed coming true: the whole of our past is indeed sliding into a fossilized simulacrum, but it is man who has inherited the evil genius of artifice which was God's. Today the virtual reconstruction of the genesis of the species is the work of human beings themselves, and it is becoming the virtual reality of our past and our future.

Not only are our fossils itemized, inventoried, interpreted and reinterpreted according to changing scientific hypotheses and fashions, but the whole thing has taken on the air of cinematic work (editing, framing, lighting, sequences, dissolves) on geological and archaeological material whose objective reality is becoming intangible. It is the same with these relics as it is with those particles in subatomic physics which have no other existence than the traces they leave on our screens.

The accumulation of traces and contradictory hypotheses leaves the same aftertaste of uncertainty, of relative credibility. The objectivity of these relics is beyond doubt. The problem is their status as reality and, therefore, as evidence, their status as objects suddenly rendered incredible by the very intensity of their itemization and the methods of analysis applied to them. These traces pass into hyperreality, as does any 'material' pursued down to the tiniest detail, all 'scientific' exploration ending up exterminating its real object.

Clearly, it is no longer God overseeing all this, as in Gosse. It is our own apparatus of knowledge, by which we are currently obliterating the traces of our existence, spiriting away the evidence for our sensible world. We have supplanted the God of *Omphalos* in the invention of a definitively fictitious past. Yet there is a difference in the ways of simulation. For though the illusionist God of Gosse had completely invented the traces of the past of the species, his creation set in train a real world and a history. Once set in place in that creation, things drift on towards their final destinations unaffected by their illusory pasts. This special effect of the divine imagination or the Creator's irony has no impact on their present state. We, on the other hand, are no longer part of reality and simulation. For us, the question of Adam's navel (which had no reason to exist since he was not born of woman, but which had to be represented in pictures so that the divine arbitrariness of the original act might be erased) no longer even arises: it is the whole of the human race which will have to be rigged out with a *trompe-l'œil* navel, in so far as there is no longer any trace, with us, of any umbilical cord which might connect us to the real world. We are born of woman still, and shall be for some time to come, but with the coming of *in vitro* fertilization we shall shortly return to the 'anomphalous' condition of Adam: future 'humans' will have no navels.

Metaphorically, we are already in the 'umbilical limbo'. Not only have the traces of our past become virtual, but our present itself is given over to simulation. It is as though Gosse's God, far more cunning and devilish than Gosse himself imagined him to be, had, as part of his inscrutable, humorous design, extended his divine simulation to the furthermost reaches of the future. Or, alternatively, this simulation of the past might not, after all, be a good practical joke, but the remorseless consequence of the generalized simulation of our present life, the logical extension of our Virtual Reality.

Beneath all this theological allegory there lie some very burning problems. It is of some consequence whether this simulation is the work of a beneficent God or the trap set by a malicious one. It is of some consequence whether the virtual illusion upon which we are entering is a beneficent illusion or whether, by moving further in this direction, we are merely getting more and more caught up in the strategem, as a result of what is, on this occasion, a deliberate choice on the part of the human race, fascinated by the idea of inventing an artificial destiny for itself. Or is it that humanity simply dreams of exacting revenge by putting the divine Creation out of joint, debasing it by systematic simulation and turning the universe into a total artefact out of scorn for the Last Judgement?

By conjuring away the process of evolution, God had protected man from an inescapable end. For, paradoxically, the only insurance against death is to have been created *ex nihilo*, which keeps open the possibility of an equally miraculous resurrection, whereas if you are the product of an evolution, the only thing you can do is disappear when your time is up. The intervention of a superior power in Genesis guarantees a future immortality, whereas the genealogy of the species condemns it, in time, to disappear. And our whole problem, in our efforts to give birth to a real world, is fundamentally the same as God's: not to drive the human race to despair by the recognition of its real existence and finitude.

For Gosse, matters are simple: reality exists on God's authority. But what can we do if that same God is capable of simultaneously creating the true and the false? (This is not even a diabolical manipulation, since the germ of the illusion came from God himself.) In this case, what is there to guarantee that our world is not as false as the simulacrum of an earlier world? All of reality – present, past and future – suddenly comes into doubt. If God is capable of conjuring up a perfect illusion of the pre-Genesis era, then our current reality is eternally unverifiable. It is not, therefore, a scientific hypothesis.

The Automatic Writing of the World

The perfect crime is that of an unconditional realization of the world by the actualization of all data, the transformation of all our acts and all events into pure information: in short, the final solution, the resolution of the world ahead of time by the cloning of reality and the extermination of the real by its double.

This is precisely the theme of Arthur C. Clarke's short story 'The Nine Billion Names of God'.[11] A community of Tibetan monks have for centuries devoted themselves to transcribing these nine billion names of God, and once they have accomplished this the purpose of the world will be achieved, and it will come to an end. The task is a tiresome one and the weary monks call in technicians from IBM, whose computers do the job in a few months. In a sense, the history of the world is completed in real time by the workings of virtual technology. Unfortunately, this also means the disappearance of the world in real time. For suddenly, the promise of the end is fulfilled and, as they walk back down into the valley, the technicians, who did not really believe in the prophecy, are aghast to see the stars going out one by one.

This is perhaps the fate that awaits us at the end-point of this technical transfiguring of the world: its accelerated end, its imme-diate resolution – the final success of modern millenarianism, though with no hope of salvation, apocalypse or revelation. Merely hastening the final term, accelerating the movement towards disappearance pure and simple. And so, quite without knowing it, the human race might, like the IBM technicians, be assigned to this noble task: triggering the code for the world's automatic disappearance by exhausting all its possibilities.

This is the very essence of the Virtual.

Live your life in real time – live and suffer directly on-screen. Think in real time – your thought is immediately encoded by the computer. Make your revolution in real time – not in the street, but in the recording studio. Live out your amorous passions in real time – the whole thing on video from start to finish. Penetrate your body in real time – endovideoscopy: your own bloodstream, your own viscera as if you were inside them.

Nothing escapes this. There is always a hidden camera somewhere. You can be filmed without knowing it. You can be called to act it all out again for any of the TV channels. You think you exist in the original-language version, without realizing that this is now merely a special case of dubbing, an exceptional version for the 'happy few'. Any of your acts can be instantly broadcast on any station. There was a time when we would have considered this a form of police surveillance. Today, we regard it as advertising.

In any case, the virtual camera is in our heads. No need of a medium to reflect our problems in real time: every existence is telepresent to itself. The TV and the media long since left their media space to invest 'real' life from the inside, precisely as a virus does with a normal cell. No need of the headset and the data suit: it is our will that ends up moving about the world as though inside a computer-generated image. We have all swallowed our receivers, and this produces intense interference on account of the excessive proximity of life and its double, and the collapsing of time and distance. Whether in this telepresence, in the live TV psychodrama or in the immediacy of information on all screens, what we have here is the same short-circuiting of real life.

*　　*　　*

Virtuality is different from the spectacle, which still left room for a critical consciousness and demystification. The abstraction of the 'spectacle' was never irrevocable, even for the Situationists. Whereas unconditional realization is irrevocable, since we are no longer either alienated or dispossessed: we are in possession of all the information. We are no longer spectators, but actors in the performance, and actors increasingly integrated into the course of that performance. Whereas we could face up to the unreality of the world as spectacle, we are defenceless before the extreme reality of this world, before this virtual perfection. We are, in fact, beyond all disalienation. This is the new form of terror, by comparison with which the horrors of alienation were very small beer.

In what was the golden age of joyful disillusionment, we carried out the critique of all illusions – the metaphysical, the religious and the ideological. Only one remains: the illusion of criticism itself. The objects we subjected to the full glare of criticism – sex, dreams, work, history, power – have taken their revenge by disappearing, producing, in return, the consoling illusion of truth. Having no more victims to devour, the critical illusion has devoured itself. Even more than the industrial machines, it is the machinery of thought itself that is laid off. At the extreme end of its journey, critical thought has wound back on itself. Where once it was future-orientated, it is now umbilical. In surviving its own self, it in fact helps its object to survive. Just as religion has become definitively realized in other – irreligious, secular, political and cultural – forms, where it is impossible to pin it down as religion (including the current revival, where it assumes the mask of religion), so the critique of virtual technologies masks the fact that their concept is seeping everywhere into real life in homoeopathic doses. In denouncing the ghostliness of those tech-nologies – and of the media – one implies that there is somewhere an original form of lived existence. Whereas, if the rate of reality is falling every day, this is because the medium itself has passed into life, has become the ordinary ritual of transparency. All this digital, numeric, electronic equipment is merely incidental to the deep-seated virtualization of human beings. And if this so grips the collective imagination, that is because we are already – not in some other world, but in this life itself – in a state of socio-, photo- and videosynthesis. The virtual and the media are our chlorophyllous function. And if we are able today to produce a clone of a particular famous actor which will be made to act in his place, this is because long ago, without knowing it, he became his own replica or his own clone, before he actually was cloned.

This whole virtual technology media circus, this perpetual 'reality show,'[12] has an ancestor: the ready-made. Those who are plucked from their real lives to come and act out the psychodrama of their AIDS or their marital problems on TV have an ancestor in Duchamp's bottle-rack which that artist similarly plucked from the real world to confer on it elsewhere – in a field we still agree to call art – an undefinable hyperreality. Paradoxical acting-out, instantaneous short-circuiting. The bottle-rack, exscribed from its context, purpose and function, became more real than reality (hyperreal) and more art than art (transaesthetics of banality, of insignificance, of nullity, against which the pure and indifferent form of art is verified today).

Any old object, individual or situation is today a virtual ready-made in so far as one can say of anyone or anything what Duchamp was, at bottom, saying of the bottle-rack: it exists, I've met it. Everyone is invited, in this same way, to present themselves as they are and play out their lives 'live' on-screen, just as the ready-made played out its role exactly as it was, 'live' on the gallery screen. And the two are merged in the initiative launched by new museums where the aim is not now to bring people to stand *in front of* the pictures – which can be done successfully, but isn't interactive enough and smacks too much of the 'spectacle' – but to stand *in* the pictures – in the virtual reality of *Déjeuner sur l'herbe*, for example – which they can in this way enjoy in real time, possibly even interacting with the work and the figures in it.

There is the same problem with the TV 'reality shows': the viewer has to be brought not in front of the screen (he has always been there, and that is indeed his alibi and refuge) but into the screen, taken to the other side of the information set-up. He has to be made to carry out the same conversion as Duchamp did with his bottle-rack when he transferred it, just as it was, to the other side of art, creating, as he did so, a definitive ambiguity between art and reality.

Art today is simply this paradoxical confusion of the two, and the aesthetic intoxication which ensues. Similarly, information is simply the paradoxical confusion of the event and the medium, and the political uncertainty which ensues. So, we have all become ready-mades. Hypostatized like the bottle-rack, our sterile identities taxidermized, we have become living museum pieces, like those entire populations which are transfigured *in situ* by aesthetic or cultural decree, cloned in our own image by High Definition and condemned, by that exact resemblance, to media stupefaction, just as the ready-made is condemned to aesthetic stupefaction. And just as Duchamp's acting-out opens on to the (generalized) zero degree of aesthetics, where any old item of rubbish can be taken as a work of art (which also means that any old work of art can be taken for rubbish), so this media acting-out opens on to a generalized virtuality which puts an end to the real by its promotion of every single instant.

The key concept of this Virtuality is High Definition. That of the image, but also of time (Real Time), of music (High Fidelity), of sex (pornography), of thought (Artificial Intelligence), of language (digital languages), of the body (the genetic code and the genome). Everywhere, High Definition marks the transition – beyond any natural determination – to an operational formula – and, precisely, a 'definitive' one, the transition to a world where referential substance is becoming increasingly rare. The highest definition of the medium corresponds to the lowest definition of the message – the highest definition of the news item corresponds to the lowest definition of the event, the highest definition of sex (porn) corresponds to the lowest definition of desire, the highest definition of language (in digital coding) corresponds to the lowest definition of meaning, the highest definition of the other (in immediate interaction) corresponds to the lowest definition of otherness and exchange, etc.

The high-definition image. This has nothing to do with representation, and even less to do with aesthetic illusion. The whole generic illusion of the image is cancelled out by technical perfection. As hologram or virtual reality or three-dimensional picture, the image is merely the emanation of the digital code which generates it. It is merely the mania for making an image no longer an image or, in other words, it is precisely what removes a dimension from the real world.

Already, in moving from the silents to the talkies, then to colour and 3-D and the current range of special effects, the cinematographic illusion faded as the technical prowess increased. No empty space any more, no ellipsis, no silence. The more we move towards that perfect definition, that useless perfection, the more the power of the illusion is lost. To appreciate the truth of this, one only has to think of the Peking Opera and how, with the mere movement of their bodies, the old man and the girl brought to life on the stage the sheer size of the river and how, in the duel scene, the two bodies, skimming each other with their weapons yet not touching, made the darkness in which the duel took place tangible. That was total illusion – an ecstasy more physical and material than aesthetic or theatrical, precisely because all realist presence of the night or the river had been excised. Today, they would pipe tons of water into the studio, and the duel would be shot in darkness with infra-red cameras.

Real Time: instantaneous proximity of the event and its double in information. Proximity of human beings and their remote action: settle all your business at the other end of the world, via an ectoplasmic intermediary. Like every detail of the hologram, every instant of real time is microscopically encoded. Every little bit of time packs in the total information relating to the event, as though it were being mastered in miniature from all sides at once. Now, there is something obscene about the instant replication of an event, act or speech and their immediate transcription, for some degree of delay, pause or suspense is essential to thought and speech. The immediate totting up, itemizing and storing of all these exchanges, precisely as occurs with writing on word-processors, bespeaks an interactive compulsion which respects neither the timing nor the rhythm (not to mention the pleasure) of exchange, and combines artificial insemination and premature ejaculation in the same operation.

There is a profound incompatibility between real time and the symbolic rule of exchange. What governs the sphere of communication (the interface, immediacy, the abolition of time and distance) has no meaning in the sphere of exchange, where the rule is that what is given should never be returned immediately. It has to be returned, but never right away. That is a serious, mortal insult. There must never be immediate interaction. It is, precisely, time which separates the two symbolic moments and holds their resolution in abeyance. Time with no delay, 'live' time, is inexpiable. The whole field of communications is, thus, of the order of the inexpiable, since everything in that field is interactive, is given and returned without delay, without that suspense, minute as it may be, which constitutes the temporal rhythm of exchange.

Artificial Intelligence. Thought at last realized, fully materialized by all the virtualities of analysis, synthesis and calculation, just as real time is defined by the ceaseless interaction of all moments and all participants. A high-definition operation: the information which results is truer than truth – it is true in real time. That is why it is fundamentally uncertain. The fact that Artificial Intelligence veers off into over-high definition, into a crazy sophistication of data and operations, merely confirms that this is indeed the achieved utopia of thought.

And now computers controlled by thought are on the way.

There is a danger that this extreme form will produce some strange results. At what threshold of consciousness or formalization will the machine intervene? There is a danger that, by reflex anticipation, it will log into subconscious – if not, indeed, unconscious – thoughts, into the most primitive phantasies. Like the double of the Student of Prague, who was always there before him, transforming his obscurest whims into acts. In this way our 'thoughts' will be actualized even before they occur, exactly like the event in the information system. If that is what we must necessarily come to, then the consequence would be that the whole system of thought would soon be aligned to the system of the machine. Thought would end up thinking only what the machine can take in and process, or would think only when the machine requests it. This is already how things stand with computers and information technology. In the generalized interface, thought itself will become virtual reality, the equivalent of computer-generated images or the automatic writing of word-processors.

Artificial Intelligence? There is not a shadow of artifice in it, not the shadow of an idea of illusion, seduction or the play of the world, which is much more subtle, perverse and arbitrary. Now, thought is neither a mechanics of higher functions nor a range of operational reflexes. It is a rhetoric of forms, of shifting illusion and appearances – an anamorphosis of the world, not an analysis. The cerebral, computing machine is not the master of appearances; it is the master only of calculation, and its task, like that of all cybernetic and virtual machines, is to destroy this essential illusion by counterfeiting the world in real time.

Just as the illusion of the image disappears into its virtual reality, the illusion of the body into its genetic formulation and the illusion of the world into its artificial technical form, so also do we see disappear, in Artificial Intelligence, the (super)natural understanding of the world as play, as delusion, as machination, as crime – and not as logical mechanism, or as reflex cybernetic machine which would have its mirror and model in the human brain.

End of the raw illusion of thought, of the scene, of passion, end of the illusion of the world and its vision (and not its representation), end of the illusion of the Other, of Good and Evil (particularly of Evil), of true and false, end of the raw illusion of death, or that of existing at any cost: all these things vanish into telereality, into real time, into the sophisticated technologies which are our initiation into models, into the virtual, into the opposite of illusion – total disillusion.

In the realm of shadows, no one any longer has a shadow, and there is no danger of treading on it and ripping it, as Peter Schlemihl did.[13] What can happen, on the other hand, is for bodies no longer to project their shadows, but shadows to project their bodies, which might then be said to be mere shadows of shadows. This is already the case with our virtual reality, which is merely the putting back into circulation, *sub specie corporis, sub specie realitatis*, of the abstraction and the digital data of life. As in that other fable where the Devil put the shadow of the student who had sold it to him back into circulation in the living form of the Double, for which the student was then merely the stand-in.

This virtual operation of the world is a paradoxical chimaera. The worldwide listing of all data is the same phantasy as that of the spelling of the names of God – a chimaera in which we bury ourselves as though inside a metal sarcophagus, in a state of weightlessness, dreaming of living out all possible situations by the grace of the Digital. Phantasy of synthesis of all the elements, by which we seek to force the gates of the real world.

With Virtual Reality and all its consequences, we have passed over into the extreme of technology, into technology as an extreme phenomenon. Beyond the end, there is no longer any reversibility; there are no longer any traces of the earlier world, nor is there even any nostalgia for it. This hypothesis is much graver than that of technological alienation or Heidegger's *Gestell*. It is the hypothesis of a project of irreversible disappearance in the purest logic of the species. The hypothesis of an absolutely real world, where, unlike Michaux's artist, we would have succumbed to the temptation not to leave traces.

This is what is at stake in Virtuality. And there can be no doubting its absolute ambition. If it were brought to completion, that radical effectuation would be the equivalent of a perfect crime. Whereas the 'original' crime is never perfect and always leaves traces (we ourselves as living, mortal beings are the trace of that criminal imperfection), future extermination – that extermination which would be produced by an absolute determination of the world and its elements – would leave no trace. We would not even have the time to disappear. We would be disintegrated in Real Time and Virtual Reality long before the stars went out.

Fortunately, all this is literally impossible. Very High Definition, with its ambition of producing images, sounds, information, bodies in microvision, in stereoscopy, as you have never seen them before, as you will never see them, is unrealizable. As is the phantasy of Artificial Intelligence: the brain's becoming a world, the world's becoming a brain, so as to function without bodies, unfailing, autonomized, inhuman. Too intelligent, too super-efficient to be true.

There is, in fact, no room for both natural and artificial intelligence. There is no room for both the world and its double.

The Horizon of Disappearance

When the horizon disappears, what then appears is the horizon of disappearance.

Dietmar Kamper

Man is constantly expelling what he is, what he experiences, what he means to himself. Either through language, which has an exorcistic function, or through all the technical artefacts he has invented and over whose horizon he is currently disappearing in an irreversible process of transference and substitution. McLuhan saw modern technologies as 'extensions of man'. We should see them, rather, as 'expulsions of man'.

This kind of energy, which tends to get rid of something – beginning, no doubt, with itself – is best encapsulated in the term 'acting-out'. Ridding yourself of your phantasies by having them pass into reality – and yet, for all that, they do not actually become real: the 'acting-out' merely expresses the impossibility of the phantasy remaining a phantasy. Projecting ourselves into a fictive, random world for which there is no other motive than this violent abreaction to ourselves. Building ourselves a perfect virtual world so as to be able to opt out of the real one. Or else, in the case of history, ridding itself of its incoherences and contradictions in a single unpredictable event, in which the actors seem mere extras – as in the events in Eastern Europe, which have no meaning in themselves, being merely the liquidation of an impossible situation. The excess of positivity, and of operational stimulation of current systems, plunges us everywhere into this kind of impossible situation where we are no longer in a position of action but of pure reaction, reflex operation and automatic response.

We are no longer alienated within a conflictual reality; we are expelled by a definitive, non-contradictory reality. Our desires expropriated from us by their very fulfilment. Absorbed and introjected and, at the same time, totally ejected. Lévi-Strauss used to distinguish between two types of culture: those which introject and absorb, which devour – anthropophagic cultures – and those which spew out, eject, expel – anthropo-emic cultures, modern cultures. But ours – our contemporary culture – seems to effect a brilliant synthesis of the two; of the most extreme integration – of functions, spaces and human beings – and the most radical ejection, quasi-biological rejection – the system expelling us, even as it integrates us, into countless technical prostheses, right down to the very latest and most admirable stage in the process: the prosthetics of thought in Artificial Intelligence.

The 'acting-out' of a whole society caught up in its phantasy of dissipation of itself in pure energy, in pure circulation, without any visible objective other than this specific feat, than this deliverance into the void, than this mobility at any cost, of which we, the living particles, the living bodies, are now merely the orbiting refuse.

We are, in this way, moving further and further from our centre of gravity (ours, the world's). And in this way we are becoming like the galactic systems which are moving apart from each other at velocities proportional to their mass. For it is only inside systems that the law of gravity prevails. Everywhere else, it is anti-gravity and negative attraction which rule. Where do we get our energy from – that energy mobilized in networks – if not from the demobilization of our own bodies, from the liquidation of the subject and of the material substance of the world?

One day, perhaps, all that substance will be transformed into energy and all that energy into pure information. This will be, in a way, the definitive 'acting-out', the total achievement,[14] the final solution. Everything will be accomplished, realized and, at the same time, ejected into the void. Delivered from ourselves, we shall enter the spectral, problem-free universe. That is what is meant by the great model of Virtuality.

Perhaps it is to escape this terrifying objectivity of the world that we are currently derealizing it; perhaps it is to escape the ultimatum of a real world that we are currently rendering it virtual. For though it lends force to existence and happiness, the concept of reality even more surely lends force of reality to evil and misery. In a real world, death too becomes real, and secretes a commensurate horror. Whereas in a virtual world we dispense with death and birth, as we dispense with a responsibility so diffuse and overwhelming that it becomes impossible to bear. We are doubtless ready to pay this price so as no longer to have perpetually to perform the overwhelming task of distinguishing between true and false, good and evil, etc. The species is, perhaps, collectively ready to reject the moral and metaphysical anguish which ensues from this and has eventually built up into a neurosis, as well as to reject the privilege of critical consciousness, and accept instead a liquidation of differences, categories and values. Perhaps it is ready to abandon transcendence and metaphor for metonymic sequences. No more polarity, otherness, antagonism, but, instead, a superconductivity, a static electricity of communication. Perhaps by paying this price we shall pass death by, in the transparent shroud of a made-to-measure immortality.

The question whether the technical project of Virtuality is a step in humanity's upward progression or a moment in its vertiginous disappearance still remains (the two are not incompatible). Might we not have invented an extremely roundabout means for radicalizing our existence by offering it a chance of total disappearance? All other cultures have left traces. *Our* crime would be perfect, for it would leave no trace, and would be irreversible.

What is the most radical metaphysical desire, the deepest spiritual joy? Not to be there, but to see. Like God. For God, precisely, does not exist, and this enables him to watch the world in his absence. We too would love, above all, to expunge man from the world in order to see it in its original purity. We glimpse, in this, an inhuman possibility, which would restore the pluperfect form of the world, without the illusion of the mind or even that of the senses. An exact and inhuman hyperreality, where we could at last delight in our absence and the dizzying joys of disincarnation. If I can see the world after the point of my disappearance, that means I am immortal. The Immortals themselves came and involved themselves episodically in the events of the world, to derive pleasure from passing unrecognized.

This might be taken so far as the staging of some collective disaster or other, merely to see what would happen. But there is nothing of the death instinct here. It is the ruse of God, eluding the question of his existence by vanishing beneath his images. It is the ruse of the original, vanishing beneath its many copies. By the very fact of existing, we are from the beginning in an impossible anthropological situation. We can nowhere test out our existence or its authenticity. Existence, being and the real are, strictly speaking, impossible. The only solution to this situation, apart from the metaphysical recourse to a higher will (the will of God, but that is obsolete), is crime. Crime stands at the beginning of all cultures, as the supreme form of 'acting-out'. And in this sense, the technological enterprise itself can be seen as criminal projection, sacrificial 'acting-out', exorcism – one of those eccentric forms which defy the gravity of existence.

Other cultures have been able to manage this metaphysical illusion by having it circulate, each person taking responsibility for the next one's life over the generations by means of rituals. Whereas we, obsessed by objective reality, unload our illusion of being on to technology. And doubtless, we play with death in technology as other cultures did in sacrifice. But this sacrifice no longer evokes the same magic or the same dreams. It is more like an experimental murder in which the murderer and the victim would be mere technical functions.

But perhaps the function of disappearing is a vital one. Perhaps this is how we react as living beings, as mortals, to the threat of an immortal universe, the threat of a definitive reality. So this whole array of technology could be taken to mean that man has ceased to believe in his own existence, and has opted for a virtual existence, a destiny by proxy. Then all our artefacts become the site of the subject's non-existence, of his desire for non-existence. For a subject without an existence of his own is at least as vital a hypothesis as that of a subject decked out with such metaphysical responsibility.

Seen from this angle, technology becomes a marvellous adventure, just as marvellous in this case as it seems monstrous in the other. It becomes an art of disappearance. It might be seen as aiming not so much to transform the world as to create an autonomous world, a fully achieved world, from which we could at last withdraw. Now, there can be no perfecting of the natural world, and the human being in particular is a dangerous imperfection. If the world is to be perfect, it will first have to be made. And if the human being wishes to attain this kind of immortality, he must produce himself as artefact also, expel himself from himself into an artificial orbit in which he will circle forever.

So we dream of a world carried along miraculously, without our intervention, and of autonomous beings which, far from escaping our will, as in the story of the sorcerer's apprentice, might fulfil the desire we ourselves have of escaping our will.

So we dream of seeing computers reach the stage of intelligent self-programming. And yet, though we concede their becoming more intelligent than us, we do not accord them a will of their own. We do not conceive a rival will in any other species and, if we are to give way to superior artificial beings, their very intelligence has to be the manifestation of our desire. Though God allowed man to pose the question of his own freedom, we cannot contemplate beings we have engendered doing the same. No freedom, no will, no desire, no sexuality – it is precisely in these respects that we want them perfect. Above all, we cannot grant them what God eventually conceded to man: the knowledge of Evil.

It seems, however, that these 'intelligent' machines have got wind, if not of crime and sin, then at least of the obscure paths of accident and catastrophe. That they have equipped themselves with a number of functional gremlins, electronic viruses and other negative side-effects which protect them from perfection and spare them, in their turn, from pushing to their limits. The perfect crime would have been to invent a faultless world and withdraw from it without leaving a trace. But we cannot achieve this. We leave traces everywhere – viruses, lapses, germs and catastrophes – signs of imperfection which are, so to speak, man's signature in the heart of the artificial world.

Not only Artificial Intelligence, but all of the advanced techno-logical process points up the fact that behind his doubles and his prostheses, his biological clones and his virtual images, man takes advantage of these things to disappear. So it is with the answer-phone: 'We aren't here. Leave a message. . . .' And the video plugged into the TV takes over the job of watching the film for you. Had there not been that possibility, you would have felt obliged to watch it, since you always feel a little responsible for the films you haven't seen, the desires you haven't fulfilled, the people you haven't replied to, the crimes you haven't committed, the money you haven't spent. This amounts to a whole array of repressed possibilities, and the idea that there is a machine to store them and filter them, into which they go to die away quietly, is a profoundly reassuring one. All these machines may be termed virtual, since they are the filter (the philtre) of virtual *jouissance*, that of the image, which most of the time is enough to keep us happy.

All these machines, which claim to be 'live' interactive devices, are in fact deferred-responsibility machines. For of course, I can see this film later if I want to, but most of the time I won't do anything about it. Besides, am I sure I want to see it? On the other hand, it is certain that the machine must function. And so the amortizing of the cost of the machine coincides with the amortizing, the deadening, of desire. These machines are all marvellous. They give man back a kind of liberty; they relieve him of the burden of his own will. They relieve him of the machine itself, as they are often interconnected and operate in a loop. They relieve him of his own production: what a relief to see twenty pages that had been stored in memory wiped out at a stroke, at a whim of the computer (or by a slip of the hand, which amounts to the same thing)! They would never have had such value if they hadn't had the good fortune to disappear. What the computer had given you – perhaps too easily – it takes away with the same ease. Everything is in order. A zero-sum technological equation. We are always talking of unforeseen, negative side-effects; here technology produces a positive (homoeopathic) side-effect. The integrated circuit loops back on itself, ensuring, as it were, the automatic deletion of the world.

To the tragic illusion of destiny we prefer the metaphysical illusion of subject and object, the true and the false, good and evil, the real and the imaginary; but, in a final phase, we prefer the virtual illusion even more – that of the neither true nor false, of the neither good nor evil, of a lack of distinction between the real and the referential, of an artificial reconstruction of the world where, at the cost of total disenchantment, we would enjoy a total immunity.

But why seek to escape destiny, to escape the order of disappearance? Out of an instinct of self-preservation? A feeble motive. Out of a defiance of the natural order and for the glory of artifice? To have the illusion of changing the world, or of mastering it? From some phantasy of wiping out origins of any kind, and substituting a self-generation stretching back to infinity?

Where can it come from, this compulsion to be rid of the world by realizing it, by forcing material objectivity upon it? Whence the idea of inflecting it, by altering even the genetic code of matter? The absurdity of this enterprise is already evident where the human genome is concerned. Once he has been deciphered and digitalized, once he has become transparent and operational, what better destiny can we invent for man? What destination can we give the world in general once we have it at our command? Physically and metaphysically, the universe has no other destiny than to be the universe itself.

In our determination to invent the real world, so as to have it transparent to our science and our consciousness, so that it no longer escapes us, we do not escape that very transparency - become now the transparence of evil – by which destiny, in any case, unfolds, seeping through the very interstices of that transparency we were trying to set against it. Once again, the crystal takes its revenge.

For a time we kept destiny and death at bay. Today, it is destiny which is surging back towards us through the screens of science. Finally, by an ironic twist, it will perhaps even be science that has brought things more quickly to a head. But of course, as in the tragic order – re-emergent at last after we had believed it lost in the comic illusion of reality – we shall realize this only at the last moment.

The sad consequence of all this is that we no longer know what to do with the real world. We can no longer see any need whatever for this residue which has become an encumbrance. A crucial philosophical problem, that of the real which has been 'laid off'. And we have the same problem with unemployment: what is to be done with labour in the computer age? What are we to make of this exponential waste? Dump it back into the dustbins of history? Put it into orbit, send it into space? It will be no easier getting rid of the corpse of reality. In desperation, we shall be forced to turn it into a special attraction, a historical tableau, a nature reserve: 'Coming to you live from reality! Visit this strange world! Experience the thrill of the real world!'

Perhaps there will one day be fossilized vestiges of the real, as there are of past geological ages? A clandestine cult of real objects, venerated as fetishes, which will take on mythic value? Already old objects seem like real ones by contrast with objects from the industrial age, but this is merely a prefiguring of the days when the tiniest tangible object will be as precious as an Egyptian relic.

We are, even now, working only for those who will discover us one day – us and our 'reality' – as vestiges of a mysterious or heteroclite age, like the skull of Piltdown Man which was a mix of the skull of a Neanderthal with the jaw of an Australopithecus. This is what will be found some day by the archaeologists of a metaphysical age, to whom our problems will have become as unintelligible as the way of life and the thinking of neolithic tribes are to us. The only problem will be one of dating and classification deep in the 'archaeological finds centres', which will have become the excavation sites of the Digital Era. Thanks to the moribund radioactivity of these few remains, some as yet undreamt-of carbon dating system will make it possible to reconstruct the genesis of all these concepts – not to mention their meaning. For in the meantime, another chronology will have been born – the Year Zero of Virtual Reality. All that preceded will have become fossilized. Thought itself is already coming to be seen as a fossilized object, an archaeological relic, itself also to be visited as a special attraction, with some 'think-operator'[15] as guide: 'Thought in real time! Experience the historical thrill of thought!'

Deep down, we are not far removed from Gosse's God who provided men with the ready-made signs of a previous history. For we are currently manufacturing the prehistory of an age which will not even remember it, to the point where all these remains will possibly even be suspected (as was the case with cave paintings in the eighteenth century) of having been fabricated at some later date by twenty-first-century impostors, depicting an obscure and, in the end, useless anthropological prehistory – that of a native wit happily now supplanted by Artificial Intelligence.

The Countdown

Reality and the real world will have lasted only for a certain time, then. Just as long as it took for our species to pass them through the filter of the material abstraction of the code and calculation. Having been real for a while, the world was not destined to remain so for long. It will have taken only a few centuries to traverse the orbit of the real, and be very rapidly lost beyond it.

In purely physical terms, we may say that the reality effect exists only in a system of relative speed and continuity. In slower societies – primitive ones, for example – reality does not exist; it does not 'crystallize', for want of a sufficient critical mass. There is not enough acceleration for there to be linearity and, hence, for there to be causes and effects. In societies which are over-rapid, like our own, the reality effect becomes hazy: acceleration brings a jostling of causes and effects, linearity gets lost in turbulence, and reality, in its relative continuity, no longer has time to happen. Reality exists, then, only within a certain time-frame at a certain level of acceleration, within a certain window of expanding systems, within a phase of 'liberation', a phase in which our modern societies found themselves until now, but which they are currently leaving behind, with reality being lost once again – as the same expanding systems undergo further anamorphosis – in illusion, though this time in virtual illusion.

Even if it is now merely an endangered masterpiece, threatened by the very advance of the sciences and technologies which ensured its pre-eminence, the reality of the world is, none the less, a reassuring hypothesis and, as such, still dominates our value system today. The denial of reality is still morally and politically suspect. The principle of simulation is still the equivalent of the principle of Evil. The real scandal is not offending against public decency but offending against the reality principle, and we are not far removed here from the medieval trials in which the gravest crime laid at the door of witches was not that of succumbing to Evil, but that of succumbing to the illusion of Evil and its phantasmagoria.

However, it is not just particle physics and the technologies of the virtual which are on the verge of disavowing reality. We all are, in our most everyday acts. The concept has taken on a kind of ghostly flimsiness, and there is abroad something of a collective, panic-stricken sense that by wishing the world ever more real, we are devitalizing it. The real is growing and growing; one day everything will be real; and when the real is universal, that will spell death.

In one of the Marx Brothers' films, Harpo is leaning against a wall. 'What are you doing there?' 'Holding up the wall,' he gestures. 'Are you kidding? Get away!' Harpo steps aside, and the wall collapses. Are we not all leaning against that wall, and is it not the wall of Reality? If just one person moved away, the wall would come down, burying the millions of people squatting this disused barracks. The situation is certainly one of a devastated reality, and there are already innumerable victims buried alive in the rubble. The point is not, then, to assert that the real does or does not exist – a ludicrous proposition which well expresses what that reality means to us: a tautological hallucination ('the real exists, I have met it'). There is merely a movement of the exacerbation of reality towards paroxysm, where it involutes of its own accord and implodes leaving no trace, not even the sign of its end. For the body of the real was never recovered. In the shroud of the virtual, the corpse of the real is forever unfindable.

Once, the two terms were linked in the living movement of a history: the actual form emerged from the virtual, like the statue emerging from the block of marble. Today, they are entwined in the notorious movement of the dead. For the dead man continues to move, and the corpse of the real never stops growing. The virtual is, in fact, merely the dilatation of the dead body of reality – the proliferation of an achieved universe, for which there is nothing left but to go on endlessly hyperrealizing itself.

We are in the speeded-up phase of that movement where all 'real' things are in a hurry to live and die. We are in the – perhaps interminable – phase of hysteresis of the real, of remanence of the shreds of reality in the immense virtuality which surrounds them, like the shreds of territory over the expanse of the map in the Borges story.

We are, in effect, persisting in the increasingly sophisticated deconstruction of a world which can no longer secrete its end. So everything is able to go on to infinity. We no longer have the means to stop the processes which now run on without us, beyond reality, so to speak, in an endless speculation, an exponential acceleration. But do so, as a result, in an indifference which is also exponential. '*Sans fin*' – without end – equals '*sans faim*' – without hunger: it is a kind of anorexic history which no longer feeds on real happenings, and wears itself out in counting down. A history without desire, without passion, without tension, without real events, where the problem is no longer one of changing life, which was the maximal utopia, but of surviving, which is the minimal utopia.

We live both haunted by the primal scene and with the threat of the terminal phase hanging over us. And this latter is in fact characterized by the resurrection of all the demons of the primal scene, which no progress or historical revolution has disarmed, just as the germs and viruses which were thought to be buried revive one by one in the terminal phase of illness.

And AIDS is, indeed, the illustration of this preordained falling-due of death. But it is merely one particular case of it: in the future we shall all be condemned to know in advance the date and detailed form of our deaths. So we shall all be in a countdown situation, in a situation of a programmed rundown of time. This stipulation of death within a finite period makes it a kind of time-bomb, a terrifying event, because it puts an end even to the prospect of its random occurrence. Hence the vitally urgent need to stay this side of the running of the programme, to de-programme the end. Now the aim of our system is precisely the opposite: to drive right through to the end, to exhaust all the possibilities.

The human race has already gone beyond its potential. Excess of potential intelligence, hypertely of intelligence. If the law of natural selection were true, our brains would have to shrink, for their capacities exceed all natural purposes and endanger the species. This is the same question Darwin and Wallace debated, the latter resolving it by the intervention of God. God was alone responsible for this supernatural privilege of man. But if God is responsible for this biological extravagance, then he is in collusion with the spirit of Evil, whose specific peculiarity is to drive the universe to excess. Are there not signs of the aberrancy of the divine will in the catastrophic success of man?

This disproportion between the human brain and the specific tasks of the species is a glaring one in the immense majority of our activities (gambling on horses, jogging, TV, not to mention 'sleaze' and politics). If 80 per cent of human genes are useless, how do matters stand with the useable power of the brain? Was it necessary to mobilize such a cortical and cerebrospinal machinery to get to where we are? Who can say why a particular person possesses an arsenal of a billion neurons? Obviously, this is a stupid question so far as his positioning within the teleonomic mutations of the species is concerned. And he can flatter himself that he is part of that mysterious proportion of useless beings (like the 80 per cent of the genes – useless for what?) which doubtless perform a function for the species as a reserve and a backup, by contrast with those hyper-brains glued to their computers which, though already considerably underused, diminish themselves even more by having a machine function in their stead.

It is the same with Artificial Intelligence and the new technologies. Computer chips have already outstripped any possible use that can be made of them, and are leading the system into insane applications. The two together – brains and human technologies – are colluding in an effort to maximize time-capital, life-capital, in which all margins, all free zones, are being wiped out. There are no longer any reserves of uselessness: these are threatened with intensive exploitation. Insignificance is under threat from an excess of meaning. Banality is threatened with its hour of glory. The supply of floating signifiers has fallen to dangerous levels. Death itself is under threat of death. . . . Once the dialectical balance is upset, the whole system becomes terroristic. We ought now to turn those lines of Hölderlin around: 'But where there is danger, there grows also what saves' [*Da, wo die Gefahr wächst, wächst das Rettende auch*], and say 'But where what saves grows, there also grows danger' [*Da, wo das Rettende wächst, wächst die Gefahr auch*], which would characterize the much graver threat of disintegration and death represented by our excess of security, prevention, immunity, and the fatal excess of positivity.

The clock at the Pompidou Centre, where the countdown to the end of the millennium is shown digitally, in millions of seconds, is a fine illustration of this virtual exhaustion. As with rocket launches or time-bombs (perhaps the Pompidou Centre is a time-bomb?), time is not counted from an origin, but is counted down from the end. And that end is no longer the final term of a history, of a progressive unfolding, but the mark of a zero-sum, of the exhaustion of a time-capital.

Humanity no longer has any finality once the human is set down in a genetic capital and the transcription of the genome. There is no longer, strictly speaking, any history or time once it becomes part of a counting-down. When you count the seconds which separate you from the end, then everything is already finished. Perhaps it is the shadow of the year 2000 which hovers over this descending count and over the enjoyment, whether in delight or in terror, of the span of time left to us.

The Material Illusion

So long as an illusion is not recognized as an error, it has a value precisely equivalent to reality. But once the illusion has been recognized as such, it is no longer an illusion. It is, therefore, the very concept of illusion, and that concept alone, which is an illusion.

This holds true for the subjective illusion, the illusion of the subject who opts for the wrong reality, who mistakes the unreal for the real or, worse, mistakes the real for the real (that illusion is quite a hopeless one). Against this subjective and metaphysical illusion: the radical illusion, the objective illusion of the world. A contradiction in terms – how can an illusion be objective? But this is precisely the point: it is tempting to take this objectivity which has for so long been deployed in favour of truth and deploy it in the opposite direction, just as it was tempting, in days gone by, to believe in an objective reality of Evil. Admittedly this was a spiritual heresy, but it was an enthralling hypothesis. And since, in any case, even our scientific objectivity is gradually taking on an illusory character these days, there is nothing to stop illusion, for its part, taking an objective turn.

The objective illusion is the physical fact that in this universe no things coexist in real time – not sexes, stars, this glass, this table, or myself and all that surrounds me. By the fact of dispersal and the relative speed of light, all things exist only in a recorded version, in an unutterable disorder of time-scales, at an inescapable distance from each other. And so they are never truly present to each other, nor are they, therefore, 'real' for each other. The fact of this irremediable distance and this impossible simultaneity, the fact that when I perceive this star it has perhaps already disappeared – a relationship which can be extended, relatively speaking, to any physical object or living being – this is the ultimate foundation, the material definition, so to speak, of illusion.

The illusion of time is of the same order. It is the objective fact that you are never entirely there at the particular moment, and that integral presence is only ever virtual. If it is true that at any point in time you are in that moment and not elsewhere, you are never at the single point where the whole event might be said to be summed up. 'Real' time does not, therefore, exist; no one exists in real time; nothing takes place in real time – and the misunderstanding is total.

This distance is vital, for without it we would perceive nothing; everything would be totally crowded together, as it doubtless was in the primal state of the world – the only state we can say existed in real time, since all matter was coexistent with itself, present to itself at a single point and a single moment. Once that initial (and perfectly hypothetical) state came to an end, the illusion of the world began. After that, the elements were never again to be present to each other. Everything began to exist but, by that very token, did so on the basis of a relative but definitive absence of every thing from every other. Hence on the basis of an irrevocable illusion.

That distance, that absence, are today under threat. What is impossible at the cosmic level (that the night should disappear by the simultaneous perception of the light of all the stars) or in the sphere of memory and time (that all the past should be perpetually present, and that events should no longer fade into the mists of time) is possible today in the technical universe of information. The info-technological threat is the threat of an eradication of the night, of that precious difference between night and day, by a total illumination of all moments. In the past, messages faded on a planetary scale, faded with distance. Today we are threatened with lethal sunstroke, with a blinding profusion, by the ceaseless feedback of all information to all points of the globe.

It's a good thing we ourselves do not live in real time! What would we be in 'real' time? We would be identified at each moment exactly with ourselves. A torment equivalent to that of eternal daylight – a kind of epilepsy of presence, epilepsy of identity. Autism, madness. No more absence from oneself, no more distance from others. Now, otherness is that happy distortion without which everyone would simultaneously be me. It is the vital illusion of otherness which prevents the ego from succumbing to absolute reality. Language, too, is what prevents everything from signifying at every moment, and allows us to escape the perpetual irradiation of meaning. This specific illusion of language, this poetic function, no longer exists in virtual or digital languages, where the equivalence is total, the interaction as well regulated as in closed question-and-answer circuits and the energy as immediately decodable as a heat source's energy is decodable by water in a pan. These languages are no more languages than the computer-generated image is an image.

Fortunately, something in language is irreducible to this computation, something in the subject is irreducible to identification, something in exchange is irreducible to interaction and communication.

Even the scientific object is ungraspable in its reality. Like the stars, it appears only light years away, as a trace on the screens. Like them, by the time we record it, it might also have disappeared. The fact that we cannot determine both the velocity and position of a particle is part of the illusion of the object and its perpetual play. Even the particles in the accelerator do not smash into each other in real time, and are not exactly contemporaneous with each other.

Modern physics offers us other schemas than that of our reality principle. This latter is based on distinction between things, yet on their correlation within a single space – their presence one to another. The schema of physics, by contrast, is based on inseparability, yet on the absence of things one from another (they do not interact in a homogeneous space). Particles are inseparable, but light years apart.

That everything is secretly inseparable, but that nothing truly communicates – that is to say, nothing passes through the same so-called real world – that all that is exchanged are singular effects from times and spaces, beings and objects which are not, strictly speaking, 'real' for each other (their 'reality-in-itself' being forever unintelligible), is the objective illusion of the world. This singularity effect applies to all things – earthly and stellar, extra-ordinary or banal, living or inanimate: our perception of them shows them to us definitively distanced from – and necessarily never getting back to – their sources.

The objective illusion is the impossibility of an objective truth once the subject and object are no longer distinct, and the impossibility of any knowledge based on that distinction. This is the current situation of experimental science – inseparability of phenomena, inseparability of subject and object. Not that of their magical confusion in so-called irrational thought, but that of the most sophisticated investigation, at the end of which one has to accept the radical enigma of the object, and its disappearance as such.

The distinction between subject and object, a fiction that can be maintained in a zone of perception that is on a human scale, breaks down at the level of extreme phenomena and microscopic phenomena. These restore the fundamental inseparability of the two or, in other words, the radical illusion of the world where our cognitive apparatus is concerned. Much has been made of the alteration of the object by the subject in observation. But no one has raised the question of the opposite alteration and its diabolical mirror-effect. Now, the interesting situations are those in which the object slips away, becomes elusive, paradoxical and ambiguous, and infects the subject himself and his analytical procedure with that ambiguity. The main focus of interest has always been on the conditions in which the subject discovers the object, but those in which the object discovers the subject have not been explored at all. We flatter ourselves that we discover the object and conceive it as waiting there meekly to be discovered. But perhaps the cleverer party here is not the one we think. What if it were the object which discovered us in all this? What if it were the object which invented us? This would give us not merely an uncertainty principle, which can be mastered by equations, but a principle of reversibility which is much more radical and more aggressive. (Similarly, didn't viruses discover us at least as much as we discovered them, with all the consequences that follow? And didn't the American Indians themselves discover us in the end? This is the eternal revenge of the mirror peoples.)

These phenomena are not confined to micro-universes. In politics, economics and the 'human' sciences, the inseparability of subject and object is everywhere resurgent where the simulated objectivity of science had taken hold over the last three centuries.

It isn't just in physics that it's impossible to calculate the momentum and the position of a particle simultaneously. It's the same where the possibility of calculating both the reality and the meaning of an event in news coverage is concerned, the imputation of causes and effects in a particular complex process, the relationship between terrorist and hostage, between virus and cell. Each of our actions is at the same stage as the erratic laboratory particle: we can no longer simultaneously calculate its end and its means. We can no longer simultaneously calculate the price of a human life and its statistical value. Uncertainty has filtered into all areas of life: it isn't clear why it might be confined to science alone. And this is not an effect of the complexity of the parameters: that problem we can always surmount. It is a radical uncertainty, because it is linked to the extreme character of phenomena and not just to their complexity. Beyond the limit [*ex-terminis*], the laws of physics themselves become reversible, and we are no longer in command of the rules, if there are any. At any event, the rules are no longer those of subjects and truth.

Since we cannot grasp both the genesis and the singularity of the event, the appearance of things and their meaning, we are faced with an alternative: either we master their meaning, and appearances elude us, or the meaning eludes us, and appearances are saved. Since most of the time the meaning escapes us, this makes it certain that the secret, the illusion which binds us under the seal of secrecy, will never be unmasked. This is not something mystical but something that arises from an active strategy of the world towards us – a strategy of absence and relinquishment, as a result of which, by the very play of appearances, things stray further and further from their meaning, and doubtless further and further from each other also, the world accentuating its flight into strangeness and the void.

While physicists seek the equations which would unify all physical forces, the galaxies continue to move apart at fabulous speeds. While semiotics seeks a unified theory of the linguistic field, languages and signs continue to move apart like galaxies, as an effect of some sort of linguistic Big Bang, but always remaining secretly inseparable.

The illusion of the world – its enigma – also derives from the fact that for the poetic imagination, the imagination concerned with appearances, it is there in its entirety at a stroke, whereas for analytical thought it has an origin and a history. Now, everything which appears at a stroke, without historical continuity, is unintelligible. None of the means by which we aspire to elucidate it can change anything of the original *coup de force*, of this sudden irruption into appearance which the will to transparency and information vainly seek to resolve.

If the world has a history, we can hope to get a final explanation out of it. If, on the other hand, it was born at a stroke, it is not susceptible of having an end set to it – we are protected from its end by this non-meaning which takes on the force of poetic illusion. Illusion, being pre-eminently the art of appearing, of emerging from nothing, protects us from being. And being also pre-eminently the art of disappearing, it protects us from death. The world is protected from its end by its diabolic indeterminacy. By contrast, all that is determinate is condemned to be exterminated.

Two orders of thinking hover around this ontological obstacle. For the one, classical and 'rational', the only hypothesis is that of an evolution and a progress of living forms. For the other, which is highly improbable (with no hope of proof), the biomass appeared at a stroke – the Big Bang of living matter – and is present in its entirety from the beginning (even if the history of complex forms was then to follow). Exactly like language in Lévi-Strauss: the logomass, the mass of signifier, emerges at a stroke, in its entirety. Nothing further will be added in terms of information. There is even too much – an excess of signifier, which will never be reduced. Once it has appeared, it is, like the biomass, indestructible. As indestructible as mass itself, as the material substance of the world and, closer to us, the sociological masses whose just as sudden and unpredictable appearance is also irreversible, up until their possible collapse.

Astromass, biomass, logomass, sociomass – all of these are doubtless destined to come to an end, though not gradually but, rather, by a breakdown which is, like their appearance, sudden. Cultures also invent themselves at a stroke – their emergence is inexplicable in evolutionistic terms. They have all their intensity at the outset, and they disappear very quickly – sometimes even suddenly, and without any apparent reason (only ours seems inclined to go on for ever).

As for the world of the mind, it functions according to the same catastrophic rule: everything is there from the outset, it is not negotiated stage by stage. It is like the rules of a game – perfect the way it is, any idea of progress or change being absurd.

And, by the same token, one cannot imagine the illusion coming about gradually, the world becoming progressively more and more of an illusion (one can, on the other hand, imagine it increasingly taking itself for real, and becoming so in its own eyes). We have, then, to propose the same hypothesis of a total, unpredictable and definitive emergence: the level of illusion could neither grow nor diminish, since it is coextensive with the world as appearance. The illusion is the world-effect itself.

This suddenness, this emergence from the void, this non-anteriority of things to themselves, continues to affect the event of the world at the very heart of its historical unfolding. What constitutes an event is what breaks with all previous causality. The event of language is what makes it re-emerge miraculously every day, as a finished form, outside of all previous significations. Photography, too, is the art of dissociating the object from any previous existence and capturing its probability of disappearing in the moment that follows. In the end, we prefer the *ab nihilo*, prefer what derives its magic from the arbitrary, from the absence of causes and history. Nothing gives us greater pleasure than what emerges or disappears at a stroke, than emptiness succeeding plenitude. Illusion is made up of this magic portion, this accursed share which creates a kind of absolute surplus-value by subtraction of causes or by distortion of effects and causes.

This machination of the Nothing, which means that things contradict their very reality, may be conceived either as poetic or as criminal. All that is unintelligible is criminal in substance, and all thinking which fuels this enigmatic machination is the perpetuation of this crime. If the world is without reference and without ultimate reason, why do you expect thought to have these things?

The Secret Vestiges of Perfection

The hope of theory is that, by impressing upon formalism a sufficiently high degree of symmetry, while preserving its coherence, it might be possible to determine the perfect equation of the world in unequivocal fashion. Once that task has been completed, it is right and proper to destroy the equation immediately.

The necessary feat of symmetry-breaking – the passage from perfection to imperfection – is accomplished in physics by a most artful procedure.

One abstracts, first of all, from the clumsy appearances of reality, to render it consonant with the canon of classical beauty, then one breaks, one by one, the symmetries of absolute beauty in order to make the model resemble the sensible appearance.

(Michel Cassé, *Du Vide et de la Création*)

At the extreme original temperatures (the hypothetical ones of the Big Bang), particles and anti-particles are produced in equal number. The prodigious formation, in a very short time, of all elementary particles and their doubles.

Then comes the expansion and cooling of the Universe – the process of materialization of the Universe slows down. Disappearance of anti-particles in favour of simple particles, without anti-matter. From this comes the 'real' world, the effect of the 'material' reality of the world. But in the beginning, this materialization involves both matter and anti-matter. It is only the eclipsing of anti-matter that puts an end to maximal density and energy, in favour of the minimal energy of reality. The cooling of the universe is accompanied by a restricted materiality, governed, at last, by a few verifiable physical laws (including, with the emergence of light, the possibility of observation, and thus of an 'objectivity' of the world).

Before this material 'objectivity', then, there is the primal void, which is defined as a space without any real particles. Not nothingness but an ocean of virtual particles, which give it an energy of its own, a potential energy, which is nothing, but can transform itself into everything that is. A capricious energy, from before the precipitation of matter into the cycle of causes and effects.

Such is the Nothing, the Void, primal scene of the material illusion, and continuation of the Nothing as perpetuation of that state. This enables us to sketch out what illusion is, as opposed to the real. Illusion is the quality of a world which, by the antinomic structure of matter, retains the potentiality of the nullification and immaterial return of energy. Illusion is the characteristic of what retains the possibility of wiping itself out by a violent reversion (matter/anti-matter abreaction) and, therefore, of passing beyond 'material' objectivity (matter and anti-matter are indistinguishable in the absolute; they shine with the same light; they are distinct, linked to each other, only by virtue of the possibility of cancelling each other out). Only energy bound to restricted materiality – to our materiality – is doomed to dissipation and entropy.

The original void is amorphous, sterile, homogeneous, symmetrical. It is perfect. No reality can emerge there. It is absolute illusion. This symmetry has to be broken if a law-governed materiality is to establish itself – an imperfection, in which real bodies emerge (but where can such an imperfection possibly come from? What sets off breakings of symmetry?). Of that imperfection, we – human beings – are the trace, since perfection is of the order of the inhuman. We are also, however, the heirs of the Void, of the Nothing, of that primal scene of absence, that perfectly indecipherable and enigmatic state of the Universe – a situation which will never be compensated for by the real and the hegemony of the real. We are the heirs both to symmetry and to breakings of symmetry, and our imperfection is as radical as the radical illusion of the Void can be.

On the further slope looms the perfect crime: the destruction of all illusion, saturation by absolute reality. All traces of the initial state are wiped away. With the venture of technology, we are embarked upon the completion of what began with the dispersion of the initial void: the annihilation of the void, of that perfect illusion, in the name of an achieved reality – the equivalent of total entropy – to be completed at some unknowable date. But this may be unforeseeably hastened, as a function of the process of increasing information. For this latter, contrary to the negentropic illusion of information theory, is itself part of entropic dissipation, of that destiny of restricted materiality, that destiny of greater visibility, transparency and hypercoincidence which takes us ever further from the initial conditions and brings us closer to the final solution.

Unless. . . . Unless, perhaps, we rediscover – coming to a deeper understanding of the essence of technology, as Heidegger conceives it – 'the stellar course of the mystery'. Unless, perhaps, indestructible illusion awaits us at the end of the process. Are we not dealing, through our hypertechnologies, with the transformation of all matter into virtuality, into information, into irradiation? And the world will be seen to have taken on force of reality, force of materiality, only for an intermediate phase, in which there was a possibility of establishing a few laws, a few physical constants that are already becoming problematic at sub-atomic level. Perhaps, in our reality effects, we are merely obeying a gravitational effect that is the opposite of the prodigious anti-gravitational effect at the origin of the Universe and its expansion. And why might that fundamental anti-gravity not still be at work? Should we not, then, in accordance with a new physics, grant primacy not to the attraction of the solid body towards the centre, but to the attraction of the void towards the periphery?

The Height of Reality

We labour under the illusion that it is the real we lack the most, but actually, reality is at its height. By our technical exploits, we have reached such a degree of reality and objectivity that we might even speak of an excess of reality, which leaves us far more anxious and disconcerted than the lack of it. That we could at least make up for with utopianism and imagination, whereas there is neither compensation for – nor any alternative to – the excess of reality. No longer any possible negation or surpassing, since we are already beyond. No longer any negative energy arising from the imbalance between the ideal and the real – only a hyper-reaction, born of the superfusion of the ideal and the real, of the total positivity of the real.

However, even though we have gone beyond the real, into virtual accomplishment, we still have the unpleasant impression of having missed the end. The whole of modernity had as its aim the coming of this real world, the liberation of men and of real energies, bent upon an objective transformation of the world, beyond all the illusions with which critical analysis has kept philosophy and practice fed. Today, the world has become real beyond our wildest expectations. The real and the rational have been overturned by their very realization.

Such a proposition may seem paradoxical when we look at all the traces of the unfinished nature of the world, the traces of penury and poverty, such that one might think it had barely begun to evolve towards a more real, more rational state. But we have to leap ahead of ourselves: this systematic practicalization of the world has gone very quickly, the system actualizing all the utopian potential and substituting the radicalism of its operation for the radicalism of thought. There is no point taking refuge in the defence of values, even critical ones. That is politically correct, but intellectually anachronistic. What we must do is think this unconditional realization of the world, which is at the same time its unconditional simulacrum. What we lack most is a conceptualization of the completion of reality.

This paradoxical configuration of an achieved universe imposes another mode of thinking than the critical. A thinking that goes beyond the end, a thinking of extreme phenomena.

Up to now, we have thought an incomplete reality, shot through with negativity; we have thought what was lacking in reality. Today, we have to think a reality which lacks nothing, individuals who potentially lack nothing and therefore can no longer dream of a dialectical sublation. Or rather, the dialectic has indeed fulfilled itself, but ironically, one might say, not at all by taking in the negative, as in the dream of critical thought, but in a total, irrevocable positivity. By absorption of the negative, or quite simply by the fact that the negative, denying itself, has merely generated a redoubled positivity. Thus, the negative disappears in substance and, if the dialectic has run its course, it has done so in the parodic mode of its elimination, by the ethnic cleansing of the concept. So we are still forced to think this pure positivity, to think the 'depassed real' (as one speaks of a 'depassed coma') and no longer the peaceful surpassing of the real or its doubling in the imaginary.

It is not certain that we possess the necessary concepts to think this *fait accompli*, this virtual performance of the world which is tantamount to the elimination of all negation, that is, a pure and simple de-negation. What can critical thought, thought based on the negative, do against the state of denegation?[16] Nothing. To think extreme phenomena, thought must itself become an extreme phenomenon; it must abandon any critical pretensions, any dialectical illusions, any rational hope, and move, like the world, into a paradoxical phase, an ironic and paroxystic phase. It has to be more hyperreal than the real, more virtual than virtual reality. The simulacrum of thought has to move more quickly than the others. Since we can no longer multiply the negative by the negative, we have to multiply the positive by the positive. One has to be even more positive than the positive to take in both the total positivity of the world and the illusion of that pure positivity.

Nothing has the same meaning any more once it has been confronted not with its unfinished form, but with its accomplished or even excessive form. We are no longer fighting the spectre of alienation, but that of ultra-reality. We are no longer fighting our shadows, but transparency. And every step in technological progress, every advance in information and communications, brings us closer to that inescapable transparency. All the signs have been reversed as a result of this precession of the end, this irruption of the final term at the very heart of things and their unfolding. The same acts, the same thoughts and the same hopes which brought us nearer to that finality we so longed for now take us away from it, since it is behind us. Similarly, everything changes meaning once the movement of History crosses this fatal demarcation line: the same events have different meanings depending on whether they take place in a history that is being made or in a history being unmade. It's the same with the curve of History as it is with the trajectory of reality. It is the upward movement which gives them force of reality. On the downward curve – or because the movement is simply continuing as a result of its own inertia – everything is caught in a different refraction space, as in a gravity alternator. In that new space, as in Alice's looking-glass space, words and effects are stood on their head, and every movement impedes every other.

The balance which, by the force of the negative, governed our world has been upset. Events, discourses, subjects or objects exist only within the magnetic field of value, which only exists as a result of the tension between two poles: good or evil, true or false, masculine or feminine. It is these values, now depolarized, which are beginning to spin in the undifferentiated field of reality. And objects, too, are beginning to spin in the undifferentiated field of value. All there is now is a circular form of switching or substitution between disconnected and erratic values. Everything which stood in a fixed relation of opposition is losing its meaning by becoming indistinguishable from its opposite as a result of the upsurge of a reality which is absorbing all differences and conflating opposing terms by promoting them all unreservedly.

With everything losing its distance, its substance, its resistance in the in-different acceleration of the system, crazed values are beginning to produce their opposites, or to eye each other longingly. And so the transparence of Evil is merely the transpiration of the worst through the best. Nothing is more entertaining than the fact that Evil comes out of Good. But isn't there an equal irony in the fact that Good comes out of Evil? We have, in fact, to look at things differently. Good is when Good comes out of Good, or Evil out of Evil. That is when there is order. Evil is when Evil comes out of Good, or Good out of Evil. That is when things are all wrong. It is as though the cells of the heart were producing liver cells. Every discrepancy between cause and effect is of the order of Evil.

The extermination of the negative is, therefore, the final solution. But the die is not cast. The destiny of the positive, of a system culminating in positivity and pure speculation, remains, itself, enigmatic. By a form of secret coherence, one finds there a kind of balance of Evil, a kind of syllogism of the Void and Absence – a dialectics of nullity.

In his *Flüchtlingsgespräche*, Brecht has two refugees in transit talking over a beer in a station buffet. Ziffer says: 'This beer isn't a beer. But the fact that this cigar isn't a cigar either makes up for that. If the beer weren't a beer, but the cigar were a cigar, then things would be all wrong.' So order is established out of the harmonious compensating effect of several disorders. This is the ironic version of the double negative. In the French expression '*bête et méchant*',[17] the fact of being nasty is harmonious compensation for the fact of being stupid – there is no longer any scandal about it; logic remains intact. We have here the subtle equilibrium of the negative, the balancing of Evil by Evil. Though this does not find an equivalent in the balancing of Good by Good, since that is the utopia of an ideal world, of the ideal good – precisely the utopia of stupidity.

So the world goes its way naturally, by a logical enchainment of Evil which seems much more capable of accounting for it than the opposite enchainment of Good.

In the same dialogue, Brecht writes: 'When, in the wrong place, there is something, that's disorder. When, in the right place, there is nothing, that's order.' So the dialectic follows its course – not towards an ideal solution, but towards a null order, and the self-evidence of the world as the self-evidence of a zero-sum equation. A *dialectique du pire*, but a well-tempered dialectic none the less. The only one you can rely on with certainty. It is a good thing, in the end, that, in the right place, there is nothing rather than something.

If this dialectics of nullity is more reliable, this is because it corresponds profoundly to the symbolic rule. Nothing is exchanged in terms of positive equivalence – the only things really exchanged are absence and the negative. Evil has to be given and returned for human beings to be bound by a profound reciprocity. Such is the economy of the accursed share, of which the nothing, the evil, the irreducible and absence are the symbolic operators.

So, when, in the right place (in the streets in May '68), something happens, there is disorder. But is there not equal disorder if, where something should have happened (on the screens during the Gulf War), nothing happens? No pictures and, strictly speaking, no war. But the non-happening of the pictures was secretly in tune with the non-happening of the war, to the point that there too everything was in order, as in the story of the beer and the cigar.

Is it better to be where you should not be, but where there is something to see (elsewhere than in front of your television) or where you should be, but where there is nothing to see (in front of the screen)?

Our critical morality tends to make something emerge in place of nothing – the subject in place of the object. But the true challenge is to be nothing rather than something, not to be there where there should be someone: a strategy of non-happening, *stratégie du pire*, strategy of illusion, strategy of seduction. There is perhaps some affectation in this, but where there is affectation, there is pleasure. The idea, on the other hand, that a thing is precisely where it should be, that something is precisely what it must be – the objective point of view of order – is inconceivable. There is no possibility of that order in a real world.

There is, at any rate, no possibility of being oneself. There is no possibility of ideas being themselves. If they come to pass, they do so disavowing themselves. Everything which becomes reality runs counter to its own concept. Thus, in the *Flüchtlingsgespräche*, it is also said that though the beer isn't a beer, though the cigar isn't a cigar, though the man is no longer a man, the passport, for its part, still remains a passport. The man is without identity, but the passport which identifies him is identical to itself. Now, the passport is also the mark of exile, and so the only thing which identifies him simultaneously bears witness to the fact that the man has become foreign to himself. In our universe of all dreams, of all desires, there is no other destiny than this disavowal of the idea, of the concept or the dream. The passport is there, but at what is, in the passport's terms, the right place, there is nothing. Things are in order.

The present world exceeds the grasp of criticism in that it is caught up in a perpetual movement of disillusion and dissolution, the very movement which is pushing it towards order and towards an absurd conformism, the excess of which creates much greater disorganization than the opposite excess of disorder.

Having reached this point, the real (if we may call it that) now responds only to a kind of objective irony and pataphysical description.

Pataphysics is the imaginary science of our world, the imaginary science of excess, of excessive, parodic, paroxystic effects – particularly the excess of emptiness and insignificance.

The existence which believes in its own existence is an infatuation, a ridiculous flatulence. Pataphysical irony is aimed at this presumptuousness on the part of beings sustained by the fierce illusion of their existence. For that existence is merely an inflatable structure, similar to Ubu's belly, which distends into the void and ends up exploding like the *Palotins*.[18]

There is irony in all extreme processes, in all processes of involution, collapse, inflation, deflation, reversibility. An irony which plays not on negation but on empty positivity, on exponential platitude, to the point where the process turns around of its own accord and rediscovers the splendour of the void.

The Irony of Technology

At the peak of our technological performance, the irresistible impression remains that something eludes us – not because we seem to have lost it (the real?), but because we are no longer in a position to see it: that, in effect, it is not we who are winning out over the world, but the world which is winning out over us. It is no longer we who think the object, but the object which thinks us. Once we lived in the age of the lost object; now it is the object which is 'losing' us, bringing about our ruin.

We very much labour under the illusion that the aim of technology is to be an extension of man and his power; we labour under the subjective illusion of technology. But today, this operating principle is thwarted by its very extension, by the unbridled virtuality we see outrunning the laws of physics and metaphysics. It is the logic of the system which, carrying it beyond itself, is altering its determinations. At the same time as reaching a paroxystic stage, things have also reached a parodic one.

All our technologies might, therefore, be said to be the instrument of a world which we believe we rule, whereas in fact the world is using this machinery to impose itself, and we are merely the operators. An objective illusion, then, similar to the one that prevails in the media sphere. The naive illusion about the media is that the political authorities use them to manipulate or mystify the masses. The opposite hypothesis is more subtle. Through the media, it is the masses who definitively modify the exercise of power (or what sees itself as such). It is at the point where the political authorities think they are manipulating them that the masses impose their clandestine strategy of neutralization and destabilization. Even if the two hypotheses are simultaneously valid, this is still the end of media Reason, the end of political Reason. Everything which will be done or said in the media sphere is, from this point on, ironically undecidable. The same hypothesis holds for the object of science. Through the most refined procedures we deploy to pin it down, is it not the object which dupes us and mocks our objective pretensions to analyse it? Scientists themselves are not, it seems, far from admitting this.

Can one advance the hypothesis that beyond the objective and critical phase there is an ironic phase of science, an ironic phase of technology? A proposition which would deliver us from the Heideggerian vision of technology as the final phase of metaphysics, from the retrospective nostalgia for being and from all unhappy critique in terms of alienation and disenchantment. And would put in its place a conception of the gigantic objective irony of this whole process, which would not be far from radical snobbery, from the post-historical snobbery Kojève spoke of.

It seems, in fact, that though the illusion of the world has been lost, the irony of the world, for its part, has passed into things. It seems that technology has taken into itself all the illusion it has caused us to lose, and that what we have in return for the loss of illusion is the emergence of an objective irony of this world. Irony as universal form of disillusionment, but also as the universal form of the stratagem by which the world hides behind the radical illusion of technology, and by which the mystery (of the continuation of the Nothing) conceals itself beneath the universal banality of information. Heidegger: 'When we look into the ambiguous essence of technology, we behold the constellation, the stellar course of the mystery.'

The Japanese sense the presence of a divinity in every industrial object. For us, that sacred presence has been reduced to a tiny ironic glimmer, a nuance of play and distantiation. Though this is, none the less, a spiritual form, behind which lurks the evil genius of technology which sees to it itself that the mystery of the world is well-guarded. The Evil Spirit keeps watch beneath artefacts and, of all our artificial productions, one might say what Canetti says of animals: that behind each of them there is a hidden someone thumbing his nose at us.

Irony is the only spiritual form in the modern world, which has annihilated all others. It alone is the guardian of the mystery, but it is no longer ours to exercise. For it is no longer a function of the subject; it is an objective function, that of the artificial, object world which surrounds us, in which the absence and transparency of the subject is reflected. The critical function of the subject has given way to the ironic function of the object. Once they have passed through the medium or through the image, through the spectrum of the sign and the commodity, objects, by their very existence, perform an artificial and ironic function. No longer any need for a critical consciousness to hold up the mirror of its double to the world: our modern world swallowed its double when it lost its shadow, and the irony of that incorporated double shines out at every moment in every fragment of our signs, of our objects, of our models. No longer any need to confront objects with the absurdity of their functions, in a poetic unreality, as the Surrealists did: things move to shed an ironic light on themselves all on their own; they discard their meanings effortlessly. This is all part of their visible, all too visible sequencing, which of itself creates a parody effect.

The aura of our world is no longer sacred. We no longer have the sacred horizon of appearances, but that of the absolute commodity. Its essence is promotional. At the heart of our universe of signs there is an evil genius of advertising, a trickster who has absorbed the drollery of the commodity and its *mise en scène*. A scriptwriter of genius (capital itself?) has dragged the world into a phantasmagoria of which we are all the fascinated victims.

All metaphysics is swept away by this turnabout in which the subject is no longer the master of representation ('I'll be your mirror'), but the operator of the objective irony of the world. It is, henceforth, the object which refracts the subject and imposes upon it its presence and its random form, its discontinuity, its fragmentation, its stereophony and its artificial instantaneity. It is the power of the object which cuts a swathe through the very artifice we have imposed on it. There is something of revenge in this: the object becomes a strange attractor. Stripped of all illusion by technology, stripped of all connotation of meaning and value, exorbitated – i.e. taken out of the orbit of the subject – it is then that it becomes a pure object, superconductive of illusion and non-meaning.

We are faced, ultimately, with two irreconcilable hypotheses: that of the extermination of all the world's illusion by technology and the virtual, or that of an ironic destiny of all science and all knowledge in which the world – and the illusion of the world – would survive. The hypothesis of a 'transcendental' irony of technology being by definition unverifiable, we have to hold to these two irreconcilable and simultaneously 'true' perspectives. There is nothing which allows us to decide between them. As Wittgenstein says: 'The world is everything which is the case'.

Machinic Snobbery

Nothing is perfect, because it is opposed to nothing.[19]

There is nothing to say about Warhol, and Warhol has said just this in all his interviews and in his Journal, without rhetoric, without irony, without commentary – he alone being able to refract the insignificance of his images and his doings into the insignificance of his discourse. It is for this reason that whatever light one casts on the object Warhol, the Warhol effect, there is always something enigmatic about him which wrenches him out of the paradigm of art and the history of art.

The enigma is that of an object which offers itself up in total transparency, and hence cannot be naturalized by critical or aesthetic discourse. It is that of a superficial, artificial object which succeeds in preserving its artificiality, in shaking free of any natural signification to take on a spectral intensity, empty of meaning, which is that of the fetish.

The fetish object, as we know, has no value. Or rather, it has an absolute value; it lives off the ecstasy of value. Each of Warhol's images is thus insignificant in itself and of absolute value; it has the value of a figure from which all transcendent desire has withdrawn, leaving room only for the immanence of the image. It is in this sense that it is artificial. Warhol was the first to bring us modern fetishism, transaesthetic fetishism – that of an image without quality, a presence without desire.

Warhol starts out from any old image, eliminates its imaginary dimension and makes it a pure visual product. Those who work on scientific, video or computer-generated images do exactly the opposite. They use the raw material and the machine to remake art. Warhol *is* a machine. He is the true machinic metamorphosis. The others exploit technology to create illusion. Warhol offers us the pure illusion of technology – technology as radical illusion – an illusion far superior today to that of painting.

Warhol's images are banal not because they might be said to be the reflection of a banal world, but because they are products of the absence of any interpretative pretension on the part of the subject. They are products of the elevation of the image to pure figuration, without the least transfiguration. Not transcendence any longer, but the rise and rise of the sign which, losing all natural signification, shines forth in the void with the full gleam of its artificial light.

In the mystical vision, the illumination of the slightest detail comes from the divine intuition which lights it, the sense of a transcendence which inhabits it. For us, by contrast, the stupefying exactness of the world comes from the sense of an essence fleeing it, a truth which no longer inhabits it. It comes from a minutely detailed perception of the simulacrum and, more precisely, of the media and industrial simulacrum. Such is Warhol and his serial hypostasis of the image, of the pure and empty form of the image, its ecstatic, insignificant iconry. He is at once both our new mystic and the absolute anti-mystic, in the sense that every detail of the world, every image, remains initiatory, but initiatory into nothing at all.

This fetishistic transmutation separates Warhol from Duchamp and all his predecessors. For Duchamp, Dada, the Surrealists and all who worked to deconstruct representation and smash the work of art are still part of an avant-garde, and belong, in one way or another, to the critical utopia. For us moderns, at any rate, art has ceased to be an illusion; it has become an idea. It is no longer idolatric now, but critical and utopian, even when – particularly when – it demystifies its object or when, with Duchamp, it aestheticizes at a stroke, with its bottle-rack, the whole field of daily reality.

This is still true of a whole segment of Pop Art, with its lyrical vision of popcorn or comic strips. Banality here becomes the criterion of aesthetic salvation, the means of exalting the creative subjectivity of the artist. Obliterating the object the better to mark out the ideal space of art and the ideal position of the subject. But Warhol belongs to no avant-garde and to no utopia. And if he settles utopia's hash, he does so because, instead of projecting it elsewhere, he takes up residence directly at its heart, that is, at the heart of nowhere. He is himself this no place: this is how he traverses the space of the avant-garde and, at a stroke, completes the cycle of the aesthetic. This is how he at last liberates us from art and its critical utopia.

Modern art had gone a very long way in the deconstruction of its object, but it is Warhol who has gone furthest in the annihilation of the artist and the creative act. That is his snobbery, but it is a snobbery which relieves us of all the affectation of art. Precisely because it is machine-like. In Picabia and Duchamp, the machine is still present as surrealist mechanicity, not as machinality – not, in other words, as the automatic reality of the modern world. Whereas Warhol identifies purely and simply with the machinic, which is what gives his images their contagious power. Other artists, even if they flirt with banality, do not have this same chain-reaction power of images. This is because they have not become true snobs. They are merely artists. Their works go only halfway down the path of artifice. Though they too have lost the secret of representation, they do not draw the consequences from this, consequences which may indeed, in machinic snobbery, involve a kind of suicide.

With Warhol we have the minimum pretension to being, the minimum strategy of means and ends. One should read Warhol's Journal – the whole of it – as the finest account of this transparency, this meticulous expressionlessness, this will to insignificance which is doubtless our contemporary version of the will to power.

Behind what some have chosen to see as obsession or urbanity:

> . . . it's all there. The affectless gaze. The diffracted grace. . .
> The bored languor, the wasted pallor . . . The chic freakiness,
> the basically passive astonishment, the enthralling secret
> knowledge . . . The childlike, gum-chewing naïveté, the
> glamour rooted in despair, the self-admiring carelessness,
> the perfected otherness, the wispiness, the shadowy,
> voyeuristic, vaguely sinister aura, the pale, soft-spoken
> magical presence, the skin and bones.[20]

This is perhaps, secondarily, why one can multiply a Warhol image to infinity, but cannot get greater depth from a detail. To my knowledge, there are no blown-up details of a Warhol work. The fact is that each one already functions like a hologram, where there is no difference between the detail and the whole, where the gaze spreads and diffuses into an insubstantial object to the point of merging with its virtual presence.

Warhol himself was never anything but a kind of hologram. Famous people came to the Factory to hover around him without being able to get anything from him, but they tried to pass through him as you might with a filter or a camera lens, which is what he had in effect become. Valerie Solanas was even to try to shatter that lens by shooting at it, to pass through the hologram to establish that blood could still flow from it. So we can agree with Warhol: 'You can't get more superficial than me and live'. And he nearly didn't come out of it alive.

Everything in Warhol is phoney: the object is phoney because it is no longer related to the subject but solely to the desire for an object. The image is phoney because it no longer has any relation to an aesthetic exigency, but solely to the desire for an image (and Warhol's images desire and engender each other). In this sense, Warhol is the first artist to have reached the stage of radical fetishism, the stage beyond that of alienation – the paradoxical stage of an otherness raised to perfection.

This is what earned him that quite peculiar form of fascination which fetishes alone attract, that fetishistic aura which attaches to the singularity of the void. And the famous fifteen minutes of fame he spoke of was only ever the ability to accede to that extreme insignificance – that insignificance which generates a vacuum all around it, and towards which all desires are thus irresistibly drawn. It is not so easy, that insignificance. In the empty space of desire, the seats don't come cheap.

Fetishes communicate with each other by the omnipotence of thought and with the rapidity of dreams. Whereas there is a deferred relationship between signs, there is an immediate chain reaction between fetishes because they are made of an indifferent mental substance. We see this in fashion items, where the transmission is unreal and instantaneous because they do not have meaning. Ideas, too, can have this mode of transmission: they just have to be fetishized.

Let us not be deceived about the cool forms, forms indifferent to themselves, which this fetishism can assume in Warhol. Behind this machinic snobbery, what is really going on is a rise and rise of objects, images, signs and simulacra, as well as a rise and rise of values, the finest example of which is the art market itself. We are a long way from the alienation of price, which is still a real measure of things. We are in the ecstasy of value, which explodes the notion of market and simultaneously destroys the art work as such. Warhol is naturally party to this extermination of the real by the image, and to such an overdoing of the image as to put an end to all aesthetic value.

Warhol reintroduces nothingness into the heart of the image. In this sense, we cannot say he is not a great artist: fortunately for him, he is not an artist at all. The point of his work is a challenge to the very notion of art and aesthetics.

The reign of art is the reign of a conventional management

of illusion, of a convention which contains the frenzied effects of illusion, which exorcizes illusion as an extreme phenomenon. Aesthetics restores mastery over the order of the world to a subject, restores a form of sublimation of the total illusion of the world, which would otherwise annihilate us.

Other cultures have accepted the cruel self-evidence of this illusion, attempting to engineer a sacrificial equilibrium within it. We modern cultures no longer believe in anything but reality (which is, of course, the last of illusions), and have chosen to temper the ravages of illusion with that cultivated, docile form of the simulacrum that is aesthetic form.

There is a long history to this. However, because it has a history, it also lasts only for a time, and it is perhaps now that we are seeing the disappearance of that history, of that restrained and conventional form of the simulacrum, and its replacement by the unconditional simulacrum, that is, a primal scene of illusion where we would meet up with all the inhuman phantasmagorias of all the cultures which preceded ours.

Warhol is the illustration of this unconditional simulacrum.

Warhol is a mutant.

At this stage of machination, of automachination, there is no longer any critical space, a space where subject and object are respectively present, but a paradoxical space, a space where subject and object have, respectively, disappeared. Not unlike current science, where subject and object positions disappear simultaneously, the only reality of the object being that of its traces on a computer screen. This new scientific space is itself a paradoxical space. There is no more a real universe behind the screens which trace the trajectory of particles than there is a subject, Warhol, behind the image of Warhol. Doubtless we no longer have art here; nor, perhaps, do we even precisely have science (what is a paradoxical science?). But this paradoxical stage is the stage we are at, and it is irreversible.

We must, then, put the interminable polemic regarding the

critical or non-critical value of Warhol behind us, the polemic about his complicity with the media or the capitalist system. Certainly, there is no denunciation in the Warhol universe, since there is not even, strictly speaking, any enunciation. That is his strength. Any critical meaning would only weaken the paradoxical position. Any negativity would merely detract from the image as extreme phenomenon, that is to say, the radical indifference of images to the world. Therein lies the secret of the image, of its superficial radicality and its material innocence, this capacity to refract every interpretation into the void. It is by preserving this indifference of images to the world and our own (Warholian) indifference to images that we preserve their virulence and their intensity.

Such is the objectless image, which lacks the imagination of the subject. Like the famous knife without a blade which lacks a handle. Instead of the handle being counterposed to the blade, as it is in the case of a real knife, in the ideal knife the absence of handle is counterposed to the absence of blade. Such is the perfection of the knife and such, too, is Warhol's universe, where nothing is opposed to nothing. That no one is opposed to no one is also, in his own terms, the perfection of otherness, because it is insignificance which binds things together, which binds people together.

Warhol is agnostic, as we all are secretly. The agnostic does not claim that God does not exist. He says: God exists (perhaps), but I don't believe in him. Warhol says: art exists (perhaps), but I don't believe in it. And it is precisely because I don't believe in it that I am the best. This is neither pride nor the cynicism of advertising. It is the logic of the agnostic. Sexual fetishism, too, is sexually indifferent: it does not believe in sex, but only in the idea of sex which is, of course, asexual. Thus we no longer believe in art, but only in the idea of art which has itself, of course, nothing aesthetic about it.

So Warhol can say: if I could be sure everything I do was just bluff, I would do extraordinary things. If I knew everything I did wasn't by me, I would do marvellous things. That is snobbery, and at the same time it is the defiant challenge of the person who does not believe in the thing that he can do it better than all those who do.

Warhol never tires himself. The agnostic isn't going to tire himself out working for the glory of God, or to prove his existence. Warhol isn't going to tire himself out proving the existence of art. Because, fundamentally, there is no need. We no more need the pathos of art than we need the pathos of suffering or the pathos of desire. A Stoic trait, this. What is good about Warhol is that he is Stoical, agnostic, puritanical and heretical all at the same time. Having all the qualities, he generously credits all around him with them. The world is there, and it's excellent. People are there, and they're OK. They have no need to believe in what they are doing, they're perfect. He is the best, but everyone's a genius. Never before has the privilege of the creator been quashed in such a way, by a kind of maximalist irony. And all without contempt or demagogy: there is in him a kind of airy innocence, a gracious form of the abolition of privileges. There is in him something of the Cathars and the theory of the Perfect.[21]

This Warholian munificence, so different from the sense of caste which is generally that of art and artists, does not derive from democratic principles. It comes, rather, from a principle of illusion (the concept of the world as the work of the devil and, at the same time, that of perfection achieved here on earth are the two fundamental concepts of the Cathars. They are also the two basic heresies in the eyes of the Church, as they are indeed today for all political and moral orthodoxies). Illusion is, in effect, the most egalitarian, the most democratic principle there is: everyone is equal before the world as illusion, whereas we are not at all equal before the world as Truth and Reality, where all inequalities are engendered.

*   *   *

This is why Warhol is able to make himself the scenarist of a perfect 'walk-on', where all are equal. All images are good, because they are all equally illusory. Everyone is wonderful, and the snaps you take of them are inevitably successful. This is the universal democracy of extras. Warhol himself does merely this: a walk-on part. Marilyn Monroe is a walk-on actor: she is a star only because she has entered pure walk-on. When she fires at Warhol, Valerie Solanas is merely one extra shooting at another. His assistants are extras, working for him, working in his stead. Everyone – and not just in the stage and media world, but in the political and moral world – is doomed to walk-on parts. What we have here is a metaphysical state of our modern world, which is akin to that of the unconditional simulacrum. The difference is that, instead of having a depressed view of this, linked to our naturalistic prejudice, Warhol delights in this walk-on state, as though it were second nature to him. A machine should be unhappy, because it is perfectly alienated. But Warhol is not: he has invented the joy of the machine, the joy of making the world even more illusory than it was before. For this is the fate of all our technologies: to render the world yet more illusory. Warhol understood that. He understood that it is the machine which generates the total illusion of the modern world, and that it is by joyously espousing this machinic 'walk-on' position [*figuration*] that he effects a kind of transfiguration, whereas art which takes itself for art merely looks like vulgar simulation.

So far as fame is concerned, Warhol's position is very simple. Fame is based on boredom, just as the aura of images is founded on their insignificance. In his Journal, the meticulous management of his fame is accompanied by a remarkable indifference to his own life. Fame is the accidental spotlight that lights up the involuntary actor of his own life. It is the aura of an existence conceived as an exceptional *fait divers*, rendered exceptional by artificial light. Everything is in the lighting. The natural light of genius is rare, but the artificial light which reigns over our world is so plentiful that there will inevitably be enough for everyone. Even a machine can become famous, and Warhol never aspired to anything but this machinic celebrity, a celebrity without consequence which leaves no trace. A celebrity which comes from the demand of everything today to be approved and fêted by the gaze. It is said that he was self-advertising. Not so: he was merely the medium for that gigantic advertising operation the world carries out through technology and images, forcing our imaginations to fade, our passions to turn outwards, shattering the mirror we held up to it (hypocritically, as it happens) to tap it for our profit.

This is why Warhol is not part of the history of art. He is, quite simply, part of the world. He does not represent it; he is a fragment of it: a fragment in the pure state. This is why, seen from the viewpoint of art, he can be disappointing. Seen as a refraction of our world, he is perfectly self-evident. Like the world itself: looked at from the angle of meaning, the world is thoroughly disappointing. From the angle of appearance and detail, it is perfectly self-evident. And so is the Warhol machine, that extraordinary machine for filtering the world in its material self-evidence.

No one can claim to describe that machine. That would imply a literal complicity, a machinic complicity, with Warhol. Now, not everyone has the good fortune to be a machine.

Objects in This Mirror

'I'll be your mirror': this is the formula of the subject. 'We shall be your favourite disappearing act!': this is the slogan of the object.[22] Yet that disappearance also has to be the 'appearing act' of the Other. For that is the only way for him to exist. What you engender in the mode of production will never be anything but the image of yourselves. Only what comes to pass in the mode of disappearance is truly other.

Beings, objects are such that, in themselves, their disappearance changes them. It is in this sense that they deceive us, that they delude us. But it is in this sense, too, that they are faithful to themselves, and that we must be faithful to them, in their minute detail, in their precise figuration, in the sensuous illusion of their appearance and their sequencing. For illusion is not the opposite of reality; it is a more subtle reality which enwraps the primary one in the sign of its disappearance.

Every photographed object is merely the trace left by the disappearance of everything else. From the summit of this object exceptionally absent from the rest of the world, you have an unbeatable view on the world.

The absence of the world which is present in every detail, reinforced by every detail – like the absence of the subject reinforced by every feature of a face. This illumination of detail can also be obtained by mental gymnastics or a subtlety of the senses. But here the technique effects this with ease. It is, perhaps, a trap.

The photo is not an image in real time. It retains the moment of the negative, the suspense of the negative, that slight time-lag which allows the image to exist before the world – or the object – disappears into the image, which they could not do in the computer-generated image, where the real has already disappeared. The photo preserves the moment of disappearance and thus the charm of the real, like that of a previous life.

The silence of photography. One of its most precious qualities, unlike the cinema, TV or advertisements, on which you always have to impose a silence – unsuccessfully. Silence of the image, which requires (or should require!) no commentary. But silence of the object, too, which photography wrests from the thunderous context of the real world. Whatever the violence, speed or noise which surrounds it, it gives the object back its immobility and its silence. In the greatest turbulence, it re-creates the equivalent of the desert, of the stillness of phenomena. It is the only way of moving through cities in silence, of moving through the world in silence.

Photography has an obsessional, narcissistic, ecstatic character. It is a solitary activity. The photographic image is irreparable, as irreparable as the state of things at a particular moment. All retouching, all repentance, has, like all posing, an abominably aesthetic character. The solitude of the photographic subject in space and time is correlative with the solitude of the object and its temperamental silence. What photographs well is what has found its temperamental identity, that is, no longer has need of the desire of the other.

The only deep desire is not for what I lack, nor even for the person who lacks me (though that is, itself, more subtle), but for the person who does not lack me, for what is perfectly capable of existing without me. Someone who does not lack me – that is radical otherness. Desire is always the desire for that alien perfection, at the same time as it is the desire perhaps to shatter it, to break it down. You get aroused only for things whose perfection and impunity you want both to share and to shatter.

Where does the objective magic of photography come from? The answer is that it is the object which does all the work. Photographers will never admit it, and always argue that all the originality lies in their vision of the world. This is how they take photos which are too good, confusing their subjective vision with the reflex miracle of the photographic act.

This has nothing to do with writing, the seductive power of which is far superior. But photography's power to stupefy is far greater than that of writing. It is rare for a text to be able to offer itself up with the same instantaneity, the same manifestness as a shadow, a light, a texture, a photographic detail. Just sometimes in Gombrowicz or in Nabokov, when their writing recaptures the trace of the original disorder, the material, objectal vehemence of things without qualities, the erotic potency of a senseless world.

Hence the difficulty of photographing individuals and faces. It is impossible to get someone into focus photographically when you can't properly get them 'into focus' psychologically. Subjects, unlike objects, are never willing accessories. They make the lens tremble. Within any human being whatever, there is such a drama going on, such a complex (de-)construction, that the lens – tempted, in spite of itself, by resemblance – strips it of its character. The problem does not arise with objects which, not having passed through the mirror stage, are exempt from all resemblance.

They say there is always a photographic moment to be seized where the most banal of beings yield up their secret identity. But what is interesting is their secret alterity, and rather than looking for the identity beneath the appearances, we should look for the mask beneath the identity, the figure which haunts us and diverts us from our identities – the masked divinity which, in effect, haunts each of us for a moment, one day or another.

For objects, savages, animals, primitives, otherness is sure, singularity is sure. The least significant of objects is 'other'. For the subject, it is much less sure. Because the subject – is this the price he pays for his intelligence or the sign of his stupidity? – succeeds, by dint of often incredible efforts, in existing only within the limits of his identity. If we can have any hope of staving off this process, it is by making people a little more enigmatic to themselves, a little more alien one to another. Thus, in the photographic act, it is not a question of taking them for objects but of making them become objects, and hence making them become other – that is, of taking them for what they are.

If there is a secret to illusion, it involves taking the world for the world and not for its model. It involves restoring to the world the formal power of illusion, which is precisely the same as becoming again, in an immanent way, a 'thing among things'.

Chuang Tzu and Hui Tzu had strolled on to the bridge over the Hao, when the former observed, 'See how the minnows are darting about! That is the pleasure of fishes.'

'You not being a fish yourself,' said Hui Tzu, 'how can you possibly know in what consists the pleasure of fishes?'

'And you not being I,' retorted Chuang Tzu, 'how can you know that I do not know?'

'If I, not being you, cannot know what you know,' urged Hui Tzu, 'it follows that you, not being a fish, cannot know in what consists the pleasure of fishes.'

'Let us go back', said Chuang Tzu, 'to your original question. You asked me how I knew in what consists the pleasure of fishes. Your very question shows that you knew I knew. For you asked me *how* I *knew*. I knew it from my own feelings on this bridge.'[23]

The Babel Syndrome

To restore the world to its pitiless illusoriness, its irrevocable indeterminacy, only one solution: disinformation, de-programming, the thwarting of perfection.

We came very close to the perfect crime with the Tower of Babel. Fortunately, God stepped in to scatter the languages of the world and sow confusion among men. For the dispersion of languages is a disaster only from the point of view of meaning and communication. From the point of view of language itself, the richness and uniqueness of language, it is a blessing from heaven – against God's secret intention, which was to punish men. But who knows? Perhaps it was all a ruse on the part of the Almighty.

Languages are so beautiful – all of them without exception – only because they are incomparable, irreducible one to another. It is by this distinctness that they exert their particular seductions, by this otherness that they are profoundly complicit. The true curse is when we are condemned to the universal programming of language. Democratic fiction of language in which all languages would be reconciled under the umbrella of sense and good sense. Fiction of information, of a universal form of transcription which cancels out the original text. With virtual languages we are currently inventing anti-Babel, the universal language, the true Babylon, where all languages are confounded and prostituted one to another. A veritable pimping on the part of communication which is the opposite of the magic illusion of otherness.

As though languages could be reconciled! The very hypothesis is absurd. They could be if they were – merely – different. But languages are not different, they are other. They are not plural, they are singular. And, like all that is singular, they are irreconcilable. We must prefer the singular to the plural. We should extend to all objects the fateful dispersion of languages.

Infected by this virus of communication, language itself falls victim to a viral pathology. It does, admittedly, suffer traditionally from rhetoric, ideological rigidity, verbal diarrhoea and tautology, just as a body can suffer from mechanical and organic attacks. The sign, too, can be ill, but it keeps its form for all that, and a critical and clinical analysis can always restore the conditions for its fitness. But with virtual languages we are no longer dealing with a traditional pathology of form but with a pathology of the formula, of a language dedicated to simplified operational commands: a cybernetic language. It is then that the stolen otherness of language takes its revenge, and these endogenous viruses of decomposition against which linguistic reason is powerless take hold. Doomed to its digital ordering, to the infinite representation of its own formula, language, from the depths of its evil genius, takes its revenge by de-programming itself all alone, by automatically disinforming itself. (The de-programming of language will be the work of language itself! The deregulation of the system will be the work of the system itself!)

Why not generalize this de-programming to the individual and the social order – extend the Babel Syndrome to the Babylon Lottery?[24]

Everything begins, in Borges's fiction, with chance being collectively put into power, with statuses, fortunes and the social game being randomly redistributed: the Lottery. As a result, each existence becomes singular, incomparable and free of logical determination. And yet – it works. Everyone ends up preferring this to the traditional social game, which was itself, in any case, also doomed to arbitrariness. Now, the objective arbitrariness of chance – open indeterminacy – is preferable to the masked illusion of free will. Everyone ends up preferring to be 'just anyone', at the Lottery's whim; ends up preferring to have an accidental destiny rather than a personal existence. We have, in any case, become 'just anyone' today. But we have become so shamefacedly, in our statistical promiscuity, our collective monotony, instead of being so with brilliance, being truly free, by a decree that comes from elsewhere.

In communication, by crowding and perpetual interaction, individuals suffer the same fate – the same absence of fate. Communication totally screens out the radiations of otherness. To preserve the strangeness between people, that personal destiny of a 'singularity of some kind' (G. Agamben), to break down that 'social' programming of exchange which equalizes destinies, all one can do is introduce the arbitrariness of chance, or of the rules of a game. Against the automatic writing of the world, the automatic de-programming of the world.

Unlike all the illusions which present themselves as truth (including that of reality), the illusion of gaming presents itself as just that. Gaming does not require us to believe in it, any more than we are called on to believe in appearances once they present themselves as such (in art, for example). But because they do not believe in the game, there is an all the more necessary relationship between the players and the rules of the game: there is between them a symbolic pact, which is never the same relationship one has with the law. The law is necessary, the rule is of the order of fate. There is nothing to understand in the rule. The players themselves do not have to understand each other. They are not real for one another, they merely partake of the same illusion, and this must indeed be shared between them – a fact which renders it superior to truth and the law, both of which claim an undivided sovereignty.

Hence the paradoxical fact of illusion as the only true democratic principle. No one is equal before the law, whereas all are equal before the rule, since it is arbitrary. The only democracy, therefore, is that of gaming. That is why the popular classes indulge in it with fervour. Though the fruits of gambling are unequal – ruled by 'luck', though this is an inequality for which you do not have to answer to your conscience – the distribution of opportunities is equal, because it is that of chance. It is neither just nor unjust. And so the people of Babylon end up preferring the chance distribution of destinies, because it leaves them free to act in total innocence. Uncertainty being our fundamental condition, the miracle of gaming is that it transforms that uncertainty into a set of rules, and thus stands outside the natural condition.

With this form of thinking based on Gaming and the Lottery, on Singularity and Arbitrariness, an end is put to the obsession with a rationalist God encompassing all the details of the universe in his vision and ruling all its movements. The idea that the slightest thought, the tiniest beating of a butterfly's wings, could be accounted for in the overall programme of creation was an exhausting situation, entailing the maximum degree of responsibility for everyone. With the Lottery and random turbulence, we have thrown off this obsession. What a relief to know that innumerable processes take place not just without us, but without God either – without anyone! The Ancients were cleverer than we are. They had bestowed responsibility for the world – for its chance happenings, its whims – on the gods, which left them free to act as they saw fit. The gods were the incarnation of the play, chaos and illusoriness of the world, not of its truth. Perhaps with Game and Chaos Theory we are casting off this historical responsibility, this terroristic responsibility for salvation and truth, which is exploited by science and religion, and recovering that same freedom enjoyed by the Ancients.

Radical Thought

The novel, which is a work of art, exists, not by its resemblances
to life, which are forced and material . . . but by its immeasurable
difference from life . . .

(R.L. Stevenson)

So, too, the value of thought lies not so much in its inevitable
convergences with truth as in the immeasurable divergences which
separate it from truth.

It is not true that, in order to live, one has to believe in one's
own existence. Indeed, our consciousness is never the echo of
our existence in real time but the 'recorded' echo, the screen for
the dispersal of the subject and its identity (only in sleep, uncon-
sciousness and death do we exist in real time, are we identical to
ourselves). That consciousness results much more spontaneously
from a challenging of reality, from a bias towards the objective
illusoriness of the world rather than its reality. This challenging
is more vital for our survival and the survival of the species than
the belief in reality and existence, which is of the order of other-
worldly spiritual consolation. Our world is as it is, and it is no
more real for that. 'Man's most powerful instinct is to come into
conflict with the truth and, therefore, with the real.'
  Belief in reality is one of the elementary forms of religious
life. It is a failing of the understanding, a failing of common
sense, as well as the last refuge of moral zealots and the apostles

of rationality. Fortunately, no one lives by this principle – not even those who profess it. And with good reason. No one believes fundamentally in the real, nor in the self-evidence of their real lives. That would be too sad.

But surely, say these good apostles, you aren't going to discredit reality in the eyes of those who already find it difficult enough to get by, and who surely have a right to reality and the fact that they exist? The same objection for the Third World: surely you aren't going to discredit affluence in the eyes of those dying of starvation? Or: surely you aren't going to run down the class struggle in the eyes of those who haven't even had their bourgeois revolution? Or again: you aren't going to discredit feminist and egalitarian demands in the eyes of all those who haven't even heard of women's rights, etc.? You may not like reality, but don't put others off it! It's a question of democratic morality: you must not demoralize the masses. You must never demoralize anyone.

Underlying these charitable intentions is a profound contempt. First, in the fact of instating reality as a kind of life insurance or a burial plot held in perpetuity, as a kind of human right or consumer good. But, above all, in crediting people with placing their hope only in the visible proofs of their existence: by imputing this plaster-saint realism to them, one takes them for naive and feeble-minded. In their defence, it has to be said that the propagandists of reality vent that contempt on themselves first of all, reducing their own lives to an accumulation of facts and evidence, causes and effects. Well-ordered resentment always begins at home.

Say: This is real, the world is real, the real exists (I have met it) – no one laughs. Say: This is a simulacrum, you are merely a simulacrum, this war is a simulacrum – everyone bursts out laughing. With forced, condescending laughter, or uncontrollable mirth, as though at a childish joke or an obscene proposition. Everything to do with the simulacrum is taboo or obscene, as is everything relating to sex or death. Yet it is much rather reality and obviousness which are obscene. It is the truth we should laugh at. You can imagine a culture where everyone laughs spontaneously when someone says: 'This is true', 'This is real'.

All this defines the irresolvable relationship between thought and reality. A certain form of thought is bound to the real. It starts out from the hypothesis that ideas have referents and that there is a possible ideation of reality. A comforting polarity, which is that of tailor-made dialectical and philosophical solutions. The other form of thought is eccentric to the real, a stranger to dialectics, a stranger even to critical thought. It is not even a disavowal of the concept of reality. It is illusion, power of illusion, or, in other words, a playing with reality, as seduction is a playing with desire, as metaphor is a playing with truth. This radical thought does not stem from a philosophical doubt, a utopian transference, or an ideal transcendence. It is the material illusion, immanent in this so-called 'real' world. And thus it seems to come from elsewhere. It seems to be the extrapolation of this world into another world.

At all events, there is incompatibility between thought and the real. There is no sort of necessary or natural transition from the one to the other. Neither alternation, nor alternative: only otherness and distance keep them charged up. This is what ensures the singularity of thought, the singularity by which it constitutes an event, just like the singularity of the world, the singularity by which it too constitutes an event.

It has doubtless not always been so. One may dream of a happy conjunction of idea and reality, cradled by the Enlightenment and modernity, in the heroic age of critical thought. Yet critical thought, the butt of which was a certain illusion – superstitious, religious or ideological – is in substance ended. Even if it had survived its catastrophic secularization in all the political movements of the twentieth century, this ideal and seemingly necessary relationship between the concept and reality would, at all events,

be destroyed today. It has broken down under pressure from a
gigantic technical and mental simulation, to be replaced by an
autonomy of the virtual, henceforth liberated from the real, and
a simultaneous autonomy of the real which we see functioning
on its own account in a demented – that is, infinitely self-
referential – perspective. Having been expelled, so to speak, from
its own principle, extraneized, the real has itself become an extreme
phenomenon. In other words, one can no longer think it as real,
but as exorbitated, as though seen from another world – in short,
as illusion. Imagine the stupefying experience which the discovery
of a real world other than our own would represent. The objectivity
of our world is a discovery we made, like America – and at almost
the same time. Now what one has discovered, one can never then
invent. And so we discovered reality, which remains to be invented
(or: so we invented reality, which remains to be discovered).

Why might there not be as many real worlds as imaginary
ones? Why a single real world? Why such an exception? Truth
to tell, the real world, among all the other possible ones, is
unthinkable, except as dangerous superstition. We must break
with it as critical thought once broke (in the name of the real!)
with religious superstition. Thinkers, one more effort![25]

In any case, the two orders of thought are irreconcilable. They
each follow their course without merging; at best they slide over
each other like tectonic plates, and occasionally their collision or
subduction creates fault lines into which reality rushes. Fate is
always at the intersection of these two lines of force. Similarly,
radical thought is at the violent intersection of meaning and non-
meaning, of truth and non-truth, of the continuity of the world
and the continuity of the nothing.

Unlike the discourse of the real, which gambles on the fact
of there being something rather than nothing, and aspires to
being founded on the guarantee of an objective and decipherable
world, radical thought, for its part, wagers on the illusion of
the world. It aspires to the status of illusion, restoring the

non-veracity of facts, the non-signification of the world, proposing the opposite hypothesis that there is nothing rather than something, and going in pursuit of that nothing which runs beneath the apparent continuity of meaning.

The radical prediction is always the prediction of the non-reality of facts, of the illusoriness of the state of fact. It begins only with the presentiment of that illusoriness, and is never confused with the objective state of things. Every confusion of that kind is of the order of the confusion of the messenger and the message, which leads to the elimination of the messenger bearing bad news (for example, the news of the uncertainty of the real, of the non-occurrence of certain events, of the nullity of our values).

Every confusion of thought with the order of the real – that alleged 'faithfulness' to the real of a thought which has cooked it up out of nothing – is hallucinatory. It arises, moreover, from a total misunderstanding about language, which is illusion in its very movement, since it is the bearer of that continuity of the void, that continuity of the nothing at the very heart of what it says, since it is, in its very materiality, deconstruction of what it signifies. Just as photography connotes the effacing, the death of what it represents – which lends it its intensity – so what lends writing, fictional or theoretical, its intensity is the void, the nothingness running beneath the surface, the illusion of meaning, the ironic dimension of language, correlative with that of the facts themselves, which are never anything but what they are [*ne sont jamais que ce qu'ils sont*]. That is to say, they are never more than what they are and they are, literally, never only what they are [*jamais que ce qu'ils sont*]. The irony of the facts, in their wretched reality, is precisely that they are only what they are but that, by that very fact, they are necessarily beyond. For *de facto* existence is impossible – nothing is wholly obvious without becoming enigmatic. Reality itself is too obvious to be true.

It is this ironic transfiguration which constitutes the event of language. And it is to restoring this fundamental illusion of the world and language that thought must apply itself, if it is not stupidly to take concepts in their literalness – messenger confused with the message, language confused with its meaning and therefore sacrificed in advance.

There is a twofold, contradictory exigency in thought. It is not to analyse the world in order to extract from it an improbable truth, not to adapt to the facts in order to abstract some logical construction from them, but to set in place a form, a matrix of illusion and disillusion, which seduced reality will spontaneously feed and which will, consequently, be verified remorselessly (the only need is to shift the camera angle from time to time). For reality asks nothing other than to submit itself to hypotheses. And it confirms them all. That, indeed, is its ruse and its vengeance.

The theoretical ideal would be to set in place propositions in such a way that they could be disconfirmed by reality, in such a way that reality could only oppose them violently, and thereby unmask itself. For reality is an illusion, and all thought must seek first of all to unmask it. To do that, it must itself advance behind a mask and constitute itself as a decoy, without regard for its own truth. It must pride itself on not being an instrument of analysis, not being a critical tool. For it is the world which must analyse itself. It is the world itself which must reveal itself not as truth, but as illusion. The derealization of the world will be the work of the world itself.[26]

Reality must be caught in the trap, we must move quicker than reality. Ideas, too, have to move faster than their shadows. But if they go too quickly, they lose even their shadows. No longer having even the shadow of an idea. . . . Words move quicker than meaning, but if they go too quickly, we have madness: the ellipsis of meaning can make us lose even the taste for the sign. What are we to exchange this portion of shadow and labour against – this saving of intellectual activity and patience? What can we sell it to the devil for? It is very difficult to say. We are, in fact, the orphans of a reality come too late, a reality which is itself, like truth, something registered only after the event.

The ultimate is for an idea to disappear as idea to become a thing among things. That is where it finds its accomplishment. Once it has become consubstantial with the surrounding world, there is no call for it to appear, nor to be defended as such. Evanescence of the idea by silent dissemination. An idea is never destined to burst upon the world, but to be extinguished into it, into its showing-through in the world, the world's showing-through in it. A book ends only with the disappearance of its object. Its substance must leave no trace. This is the equivalent of a perfect crime. Whatever its object, writing must make the illusion of that object shine forth, must make it an impenetrable enigma – unacceptable to the *Realpolitiker* of the concept. The objective of writing is to alter its object, to seduce it, to make it disappear for itself. Writing aims at a total resolution – a poetic resolution, as Saussure would have it, that resolution indeed of the rigorous dispersal of the name of God.

Contrary to what is said about it (the real is what resists, what all hypotheses run up against), reality is not very solid and seems predisposed, rather, to retreat in disorder. Whole swathes of reality are collapsing, as in the collapse of Baliverna (Buzzati), where the slightest flaw produces a chain reaction. We find decomposed remnants of it everywhere, as in Borges's 'Of Exactitude in Science'.[27]

Not only does it no longer put up any resistance against those who denounce it, but it even eludes those who take its side. This is perhaps a way of exacting vengeance on its partisans: by throwing them back on their own desire. In the end, it is perhaps more a sphinx than a bitch.

More subtly, it wreaks vengeance on those who deny it by paradoxically proving them right. When the most cynical, most provocative hypothesis is verified, the trick really is a low one;

you are disarmed by the lamentable confirmation of your words by an unscrupulous reality.

So, for example, you put forward the idea of simulacrum, without really believing in it, even hoping that the real will refute it (the guarantee of scientificity for Popper).

Alas, only the fanatical supporters of reality react; reality, for its part, does not seem to wish to prove you wrong. Quite to the contrary, every kind of simulacrum parades around in it. And reality, filching the idea, henceforth adorns itself with all the rhetoric of simulation. It is the simulacrum which ensures the continuity of the real today, the simulacrum which now conceals not the truth, but the fact that there isn't any – that is to say, the continuity of the nothing.

Such is the paradox of all thought which disputes the validity of the real: when it sees itself robbed of its own concept. Events, bereft of meaning in themselves, steal meaning from us. They adapt to the most fantastical hypotheses, just as natural species and viruses adapt to the most hostile environments. They have an extraordinary mimetic capacity: no longer is it theories which adapt to events, but the reverse. And, in so doing, they mystify us, for a theory which is verified is no longer a theory. It's terrifying to see the idea coincide with the reality. These are the death-throes of the concept. The epiphany of the real is the twilight of its concept.

We have lost that lead which ideas had over the world, that distance which meant that an idea remained an idea. Thought has to be exceptional, anticipatory and at the margin – has to be the projected shadow of future events. Today, we are lagging behind events. They may sometimes give the impression of receding; in fact, they passed us long ago. The simulated disorder of things has moved faster than we have. The reality effect has succumbed to acceleration – anamorphosis of speed. Events, in their being, are never behind themselves, are always out ahead of their meaning. Hence the delay of interpretation, which is now merely the retrospective form of the unforeseeable event.

What are we to do, then? What becomes of the heterogeneity of thought in a world won over to the craziest hypotheses? When everything conforms, beyond even our wildest hopes, to the ironic, critical, alternative, catastrophic model?

Well, that is paradise: we are beyond the Last Judgement, in immortality. The only problem is to survive there. For there the irony, the challenging, the anticipation, the maleficence come to an end, as inexorably as hope dies at the gates of hell. And it is indeed there that hell begins, the hell of the unconditional realization of all ideas, the hell of the real. You can see why, as Adorno says, concepts prefer to scupper themselves rather than reach that point.

Something else has been stolen from us: indifference. The power of indifference, which is the quality of the mind, as opposed to the play of differences, which is the characteristic of the world. Now, this has been stolen from us by a world grown indifferent, as the extravagance of thought has been stolen from us by an extravagant world. When things, events, refer one to another and to their undifferentiated concept, then the equivalence of the world meets and cancels out the indifference of thought – and we have boredom. No more altercations; nothing at stake. It is the parting of the dead sea.

How fine indifference was in a world that was not indifferent – in a different, convulsive, contradictory world, a world with issues and passions! That being the case, indifference immediately became an issue and a passion itself. It could pre-empt the indifference of the world, and turn that pre-emption into an event. Today, it is difficult to be more indifferent to their reality than the facts themselves, more indifferent to their meaning than images. Our operational world is an apathetic world. Now, what good is it being passionless in a world without passion, or detached in a world without desire?

It is not a question of defending radical thought. Every idea one defends is presumed guilty, and every idea that cannot defend itself deserves to disappear. On the other hand, one must fight all charges of irresponsibility, nihilism or despair. Radical thought is never depressive. On this point, there is total misunderstanding. Ideological and moralistic critique, obsessed with meaning and content, obsessed with the political finality of discourse, never takes into account writing, the act of writing, the poetic, ironic, allusive force of language, of the juggling with meaning. It does not see that the resolution of meaning is to be found there – in the form itself, the formal materiality of expression.

Meaning, for its part, is always unhappy. Analysis is, by definition, unhappy, since it is born of critical disillusionment. But language, for its part, is happy, even when referring to a world without illusion and without hope. That might even be the definition of a radical thinking: a happy form and an intelligence without hope.

Critics, being unhappy by nature, always choose ideas as their battleground. They do not see that if discourse always tends to produce meaning, language and writing, for their part, always create illusion – they are the living illusion of meaning, the resolution of the infelicity of meaning by the felicity of language. And this is surely the only political – or transpolitical – act that can be accomplished by the person who writes.

As for ideas, everyone has them. More than they need. What counts is the poetic singularity of the analysis. That alone can justify writing, not the wretched critical objectivity of ideas. There never will be any resolving the contradictoriness of ideas, except in the energy and felicity of language. 'I do not paint sadness and loneliness,' says Hopper. 'What I wanted to do was to paint sunlight on the side of a house.'

At any rate, better a despairing analysis in felicitous language than an optimistic analysis in an infelicitous language that is maddeningly tedious and demoralizingly platitudinous, as is most often the case. The absolute tediousness secreted by that idealistic, voluntaristic thought is the secret sign of its despair – as regards both the world and its own discourse. That is where true depressive thought is to be found, among those who speak only of the transcending and transforming of the world, when they are incapable of transfiguring their own language.

Radical thought is a stranger to all resolving of the world in the direction of an objective reality and its deciphering. It does not decipher. It anagrammatizes, it disperses concepts and ideas and, by its reversible sequencing, takes account both of meaning and of the fundamental illusoriness of meaning. Language takes account of the very illusion of language as definitive stratagem and, through it, of the illusion of the world as infinite trap, as seduction of the mind, as spiriting away of all our mental faculties. While it is a vehicle of meaning, it is at the same time a super-conductor of illusion and non-meaning. Language is merely the involuntary accomplice of communication – by its very form it appeals to the spiritual and material imagination of sounds and rhythm, to the dispersal of meaning in the event of language. This passion for artifice, for illusion, is the passion for undoing that too-beauteous constellation of meaning. And for letting the imposture of the world show through, which is its enigmatic function, and the mystification of the world, which is its secret. While at the same time letting its own imposture show through – the impostor, not the *composteur* [composing stick] of meaning. This passion has the upper hand in the free and witty use of language, in the witty play of writing. Where that artifice is not taken into account, not only is its charm lost, but the meaning itself cannot be resolved.

Cipher, do not decipher. Work over the illusion. Create illusion to create an event. Make enigmatic what is clear, render unintelligible what is only too intelligible, make the event itself unreadable. Accentuate the false transparency of the world to spread a terroristic confusion about it, or the germs or viruses of a radical illusion – in other words, a radical disillusioning of the real. Viral, pernicious thought, corrosive of meaning, generative of an erotic perception of reality's turmoil.

Promote a clandestine trade in ideas, of all inadmissible ideas, of unassailable ideas, as the liquor trade had to be promoted in the 1930s. For we are already in a state of full-scale prohibition. Thought has become an extremely rare commodity, prohibited and prohibitive, which has to be cultivated in secret places following esoteric rules.

Everything must take place in secret. We shall take the view that the official thought market is universally corrupt and implicated in the prohibition of thought by the dominant clerisy. Every intervention by critical, enlightened and right-thinking intellectuals, all of them politically correct even when they do not know it, will be considered vacuous and shameful.

Eradicate within oneself every trace of the intellectual conspiracy. Spirit away the reality file to wipe out all its conclusions. It is, in fact, reality which is fomenting its own disavowal, preparing its own ruin by way of our lack of reality. Hence the feeling that this whole affair – the world, thought and language – has come from elsewhere, and might disappear as though by magic. For the world does not seek to exist more, nor to persist in existing. It seeks, rather, the wittiest way to escape reality. It seeks, by way of thought, what can lead it to its doom.

The absolute rule is to give back more than you were given. Never less, always more. The absolute rule of thought is to give back the world as it was given to us – unintelligible. And, if possible, to render it a little more unintelligible.

The Other Side Of The Crime

With the Virtual, we enter not only upon the era of the liquidation of the Real and the Referential, but that of the extermination of the Other.

It is the equivalent of an ethnic cleansing which would not just affect particular populations but unrelentingly pursue all forms of otherness.

The otherness of death – staved off by unrelenting medical intervention.

Of the face and the body – run to earth by plastic surgery.

Of the world – dispelled by Virtual Reality.

Of every one [chacun] – which will one day be abolished by the cloning of individual cells.

And, quite simply, of the other, currently undergoing dilution in perpetual communication.

If information is the site of the perfect crime against reality, communication is the site of the perfect crime against otherness.

No more other: communication.
No more enemy: negotiation.
No more predators: conviviality.
No more negativity: absolute positivity.
No more death: the immortality of the clone.
No more otherness: identity and difference.
No more seduction: sexual in-difference.

No more illusion: hyperreality, Virtual Reality.
No more secret: transparency.
No more destiny.

The perfect crime.

The World Without Women

The World Without Women (*Il Mondo senza Donne*, 1935) by Virgilio Martini describes the ravages of a mysterious illness (eventually named 'fallopitis') which decimates all childbearing women between puberty and the menopause. The symptoms of the illness irresistibly evoke those of AIDS some fifty years later. By an amazing coincidence, it begins in Haiti and spreads throughout the world and, by another paradoxical coincidence, it is eventually discovered that this illness, which science is powerless to control (exactly as with AIDS), originated in a plot hatched by homosexuals to exterminate the female of the species! The epidemic runs its course, all adolescent girls and young women disappear, and the human race is soon threatened with extinction. The rest of the book, full of dramatic twists and turns, carries on rather like a thriller. But the central idea is that of an extermination of femaleness – a terrifying allegory of the extermination of all otherness, for which the feminine is the metaphor and, perhaps, more than the metaphor.

What we ourselves have fallen victim to – and by no means allegorically – is a virus destructive of otherness. And we may predict that – even more than in the case of AIDS – no science will be able to protect us from this viral pathology which, by dint of antibodies and immune strategies, aims at the extinction, pure and simple, of the other. Though, for the moment, this virus does not affect the biological reproduction of the species, it affects an even more fundamental function, that of the symbolic reproduction of the other, favouring, rather, a cloned, asexual reproduction of the species-less individual. For to be deprived of the other is to be deprived of sex, and to be deprived of sex is to be deprived of symbolic belonging to any species whatsoever.

On its appearance in Italy (in 1953 – it was left unpublished for twenty years, as no publisher would take it) the book was condemned and withdrawn from circulation on grounds of obscenity, though in point of fact there is nothing less pornographic than a world without women. But that was merely an alibi to conceal, under cover of a destruction of femaleness, the panic idea of a yet more monstrous destruction – the idea of a world given over entirely to the selfsame [*le Même*].

This is the literal end of alienation. There is no one on the other side any more. In the past we would have seen this as the ideal goal of the subject – total appropriation of and control over oneself. Today we can see that alienation protected us from something worse: from the definitive loss of the other, from the expropriation of the other by the same.

In German, there are two apparently synonymous terms with a very significant distinction between them. '*Verfremdung*' means becoming other, becoming estranged from oneself – alienation in the literal sense. '*Entfremdung*', by contrast, means to be dispossessed of the other, to lose all otherness. Now, it is much more serious to be dispossessed of the other than of oneself. Being deprived of the other is worse than alienation: a lethal change, by liquidation of the dialectical opposition itself. An irrevocable destabilization, that of the subject without object, of the same without other – definitive stasis and metastasis of the Same. A tragic destiny for individuals and for our – self-programming and self-referential – systems: no more adversaries, no more hostile environments – no environment at all any longer, no more exteriority. This is like wresting a species away from its natural predators. No longer threatened by them, it cannot but destroy itself (by 'depredation', as it were). Death being the great natural predator, a species we attempt at all costs to immortalize and wrest away from death – as we do with all our replacement technologies for the body's organs – is doomed to disappear. The best strategy for bringing about someone's ruin is to eliminate everything which threatens him, thus causing him to lose all his defences, and it is this strategy we are applying to ourselves. By eliminating the other in all its forms (illness, death, negativity, violence, strangeness), not to mention racial and linguistic differences, by eliminating all singularities in order to radiate total positivity, we are eliminating ourselves.

We have fought negativity and death, rooting out evil in all its forms. By eliminating the work of the negative, we have unleashed positivity, and that is what has become lethal today. By setting off the chain reaction of the positive, we have at the same time – by a perverse, but perfectly coherent effect – released an intense viral pathology. For a virus, far from being negative, is the product, rather, of an ultra-positivity of which it is the lethal embodiment. This had escaped us, as had the metamorphoses of evil which follow the advances of reason about like a shadow.

This paradigm of the subject without object, of the subject without other, can be seen in all that has lost its shadow and become transparent to itself. Even in devitalized substances: in sugar without calories, salt without sodium, life without spice, effects without causes, wars without enemy, passions without object, time without memory, masters without slaves, or the slaves without masters we have become.

What becomes of a master without a slave? He ends up terrorizing himself. And of a slave without a master? He ends up exploiting himself. The two are conjoined today in the modern form of voluntary servitude: enslavement to data systems and calculation systems – total efficiency, total performance. We

113

have become masters – at least virtual masters – of this world, but the object of that mastery, the finality of that mastery, have disappeared.

The Surgical Removal of Otherness

This liquidation of the Other is accompanied by an artificial synthesis of otherness – a radical cosmetic surgery of which cosmetic surgery on faces and bodies is merely a symptom. For the crime is perfect only when even the traces of the destruction of the Other have disappeared.

With modernity, we enter the age of the production of the other. The aim is no longer to kill the other, devour it, seduce it, vie with it, love it or hate it, but, first, to produce it. It is no longer an object of passion, it is an object of production.

Perhaps, in its irreducible singularity, the Other has become dangerous or unbearable, and its seduction has to be exorcized? Perhaps, quite simply, otherness and the dual relation progressively disappear with the rise of individual values? The fact remains that otherness does come to be in short supply and, for want of living otherness as destiny, the Other has to be produced imperatively as difference. This also goes for the body, sex and social relations. It is to escape the world as destiny, the body as destiny, sex (and the opposite sex) as destiny, that the production of the Other as difference is invented. It is the same with sexual difference. To wish to disentangle the inextricable otherness of male and female, to restore each to its specificity and difference, is an absurdity. Yet this is the absurdity of our sexual culture of liberation and emancipation of desire. Each sex with its anatomical and psychological characteristics, with its own desire and all the irresolvable dramas that ensue, including the ideology of sex and the utopia of a difference based both in right and in nature.

This invention of difference coincides with the invention of a new image of woman, and thus a change of sexual paradigm. That change, on the threshold of modernity, at the turn of the nineteenth century, was the production by male hysteria of an imagining of woman in place of her stolen femininity (Christina von Braun, *Nicht-Ich*, 1985; and *Die schamlose Schönheit des Vergangenen*, 1989). In this hysterical configuration, it was to some extent the femininity of man which was projected into woman, shaping her as ideal figure in his likeness. The point was no longer, as in the courtly and aristocratic figure of seduction, to conquer woman, to seduce or be seduced by her, but to produce her as realized utopia – ideal woman or *femme fatale*, a hysterical and supernatural metaphor. The staging of this ideal was the work of Romantic Eros: woman as projective resurrection of the selfsame, a twin-like, almost incestuous figure – an artefact doomed from that point on to amorous confusion, that is, to a pathos of the ideal resemblance between beings and sexes. The sexual difference, the concept of sexual difference which was established in the same movement, was merely a variant of the incestuous form. In that concept, man and woman were no longer anything but the mirroring [*mirage*] of each other. They were separated and different only the better to become the – often indifferent – mirrors of each other. The whole machinery of eroticism was turned on its head, since the erotic attraction which formerly emanated from strangeness and otherness now shifted over to emanate from similarity and likeness.

So Martini's *Il Mondo senza Donne* is not as allegorical as all that. By the invention of a femaleness which makes woman superfluous, makes her a supplemental incarnation, woman really has disappeared – if not physically, then at least beneath a substitute femininity.

* * *

Moreover, this goes for man too, since it is his own stolen femininity that he transposes into the theatrical mirror of the role and idea of woman. And if the real woman seems to disappear in this hysterical invention, we have to see that male desire also becomes entirely problematic, since it is now capable only of projecting itself into its image, and thus becoming purely speculative.

All the endless commentaries on the sexual privilege of the masculine gender are thus mere foolishness. There is, in the sexual illusion of our time, a kind of immanent justice which means that, in this *trompe-l'œil* difference, both sexes lose their singularity equally, their difference culminating inexorably in non-differentiation. The process of extrapolation of the Selfsame and twinning of the sexes (if twinhood is such a topical theme, this is because it reflects this mode of libidinal cloning) results in a progressive assimilation which goes so far as to render sexuality a useless function. Here anticipating the clones of the future, who will be sexed to no purpose, since sexuality will no longer be needed for their reproduction.

The coming of the problematic of gender, now taking over from that of sex, illustrates this progressive dilution of the sexual function. This is the era of the Transsexual, where the conflicts linked to difference – and even the biological and anatomical signs of difference – survive long after the real otherness of the sexes has disappeared.

When the sexes eye each other up, squint out through each other's eyes. The male eyes up the female, the female eyes up the male. This is no longer the seductive gaze but a generalized sexual strabismus, reflecting that of moral and cultural values: the true eyes up the false, the beautiful eyes up the ugly, good eyes up evil, and vice versa. They each 'lock on to' the other in an attempt to misappropriate its distinctive signs. But both are in fact in league to short-circuit difference. They function like communicating vessels, according to the new machinic rituals of switching or commutation. The utopia of sexual difference ends in the switching of sexual poles, and in interactive exchange. Instead of a dual relation, sex becomes a reversible function. In place of alterity, an alternating current.

It is in seduction, in illusion, in artifice that there is the maximum intensity, that each sex is *fatal* for the other, that is, the bearer of a radical otherness. In naturalistic terms, by contrast – the terms on which our difference and, consequently, our 'liberation' are based – the sexes are less different than is commonly thought. They tend, rather, to merge, or even to change places. What is 'liberated' is precisely not their singularity but their relative conflation and, of course, once the orgy and the ecstasy of desire are over, their respective indifference. Where do we find talk of passion now? It would seem that we talk, rather, of sexual compassion. We don't even hear much talk of desire. That rapidly declined in the firmament of concepts. It has become the astral theme of a stereotyped jargon of psychoanalysis and advertising.

Liberation is always naturalistic: it naturalizes desire as function, as energy, as libido. And that naturalization of pleasures and differences leads just as 'naturally' to the loss of the sexual illusion. Sex removed from artifice, illusion and seduction, and restored to its conscious or unconscious economy (you would have to be very clever indeed to say whether this was the 'reality' of sex). Woman wrested from her artificial condition and restored to her natural being, her 'legitimate' status as sexual being and, at the same time, to formal recognition. Now, seduction and passion care nothing for the recognition of the other. And singularity has nothing to do with identity or difference – its mode of action is singular and illegal, and that's all there is to it. Recognition goes with difference, and both are bourgeois virtues.

In any case, in this whole business about difference, there is always one term more different than the other. Woman is, in fact, more different than man. And not only more different than him, but more than different. Man is only different, but woman is other: strange, absent, enigmatic, antagonistic. And it was to conjure away this radical otherness that biological difference, and also psychological, ideological and political difference, and so on, were invented. These things can all be worked out in terms of an ordered opposition, albeit one conceived in terms of relations of force. But, strictly speaking, the opposition does not exist. It is merely the substitution of a symmetrical, differential form for a dual, dissymmetrical one. In other words, this form of 'natural' compromise is as fragile as can be. You cannot trust nature.

The *femme fatale* is never *fatale* as a natural element, but as artifice, as seductress or as the projective artefact of male hysteria. The absent woman, ideal or diabolic, but always fetishized, that constructed woman, that machinic Eve, that mental object, scoffs at the difference of the sexes. She scoffs at desire and the subject of desire. More feminine than the feminine: the woman-object. Yet we are not dealing with alienation here but with a mental object, a pure object (which does not take itself for a subject), a being which is unreal, fake, cerebral, a devourer of grey and libidinal matter. Through her, it is sex which denies sexual difference, it is desire itself which lays a trap for itself, the object which takes its revenge. The woman-object, the *femme fatale*, plays on that hysterical femininity which is masculine in essence. She plays on that speculative image by an unconditional speculation, by an inflation of her own image. By overbidding her condition as object, she becomes 'fatal' for herself, and this is how she becomes so for others. In the very features of the artificial ideal which has been manufactured for her, it is the feminine which shows through – not to meet up again with the 'real' woman she is supposed to be, but to distance her yet further from her nature, and make of that artifice a triumphant destiny.

But the sexes have asymmetrical destinies. It is not possible for man to take this same 'double or quits' option with the ideal type of virility imposed on him. He cannot raise his bid, but only let go of some of his cards. And if there are fewer and fewer

femmes fatales, this is because there aren't even any men for them
to prey on.

This respective hystericization of roles is, in any case,
diminishing as belief in nature fades in the contemporary period
and as, with its 'liberation', the problematic and ambiguous
character of this difference becomes glaringly obvious. Hysteria
was sexuality's last form of fatal strategy. It is not by chance,
then, that it is disappearing today, after fomenting all the extreme
figures of the sexual mythology of a whole century. Fatal strategies
step aside before the final solution.

A new spectrum of dispersion has appeared and, in this low-
definition sexual game, it does indeed seem that we are sliding
from ecstasy to metastasis, the metastasis of countless little
dispositifs of libidinal transfusion and perfusion – micro-scenarios
of unsexuality and transsexuality in all its forms. Resolution of
sex into its *disjecta membra*, its part-objects, its fractal elements.

The only alternative, in these new sexual conditions of indifference,
would seem to lie with woman. Because she herself wishes to
produce herself as different, because she no longer wishes to be
produced as such by male hysteria, it is incumbent upon her
to produce the other in return, to produce a new figure of the
other as object of seduction, as the male succeeded in doing to
some extent in producing a culture of the seductive image of woman.
We have here the problem of a woman, having once become a
subject of desire, no longer finding the other she could desire as
such (part of the more general problem of our age of achieving
subjecthood in a world in which, in the interim, the object has
disappeared). For the secret never lies in the equivalent exchange
of desires, under the sign of egalitarian difference; it lies in inventing
the other who will be able to play on – and make sport of – my
own desire, defer it, suspend it, and thus arouse it indefinitely. Is
the female gender capable today of producing – since it no longer
wishes to personify it – this same seductive otherness? Is the female
gender still hysterical enough to invent the other?

It seems, unfortunately, that we are coming close to the opposite extreme – that is to say, to the exacerbated form of difference or, in other words, the final solution: sexual harassment. The ultimate development of female hysteria – pornography being the ultimate and caricatural development of male hysteria. These are, basically, the two sides of the same hysterical indifference.

Sexual harassment: phobic caricature of every sexual approach, unconditional refusal to seduce and be seduced. Is this compulsion merely the alibi of indifference or does it, like all allergic symptoms, conceal a hypersensitivity to the other? The fact remains that the slightest hint of seduction, any expression of desire, is met by a charge of rape. There would be a presumption of rape at every stage in the relationship, even a conjugal relationship, if it is not expressly consented to. Italian law regards inducement as an offence – that is to say, not forcing oneself on the other to provoke their desire, nor even to seduce them, but the mere fact of inducing their consent by some gesture or sign or other. If we are to take this attitude, we should put the sperm on the blacklist too, since its effort to penetrate the ovum is surely the prototype of sexual harassment (though perhaps there is inducement on the part of the ovary?).

Where does rape begin, where does sexual harassment begin? Once we have marked out the demarcation line of an unassailable difference between the sexes, there is no longer any possibility of their coming together except in violence. So, in Bellochio's film *The Sentence* [*La Condanna*], the question is whether the man really raped the woman, since she had an orgasm. The prosecution claims that he did, while the defence's plea is that, in the end, the victim consented. But no one asks whether the orgasm wasn't an aggravating circumstance. One may in fact argue that forcing the other to have pleasure, to feel rapture, is indeed the height of rape, and more serious than forcing the other to give you pleasure. At any rate, this brings out the absurdity of this entire problematic. Sexual harassment marks the arrival on the scene of an impotent, victim's sexuality, a sexuality impotent to constitute itself either as object or as subject of desire in its paranoid wish for identity and difference. It is no longer decency that is threatened with violation, but sex or, rather, sexist idiocy, which 'takes the law into its own hands'.

At the same time, this illustrates the dead-end of difference. The problem of difference is insoluble, for the simple reason that the terms involved are not different but incomparable. The terms we are used to setting in opposition to each other are quite simply incompatible, which means that the concept of difference has no meaning. Thus, Female and Male are two incomparable terms, and if there is, deep down, no sexual difference, this is because the two sexes are not opposable.

This goes for all the traditional oppositions. We can say the same of Good and Evil. They are not on the same plane, and it is an illusion to oppose them. The real problem [*le mal*] is precisely the strangeness, the imperviousness of Good and Evil [*le Mal*] to each other, which means there is no reconciling, no superseding them, and thus no ethical solution to the problem of their opposition. The inexorable otherness of Evil passes across the ecliptic of morality. The same goes for freedom in its grapplings with information – the leitmotiv of our media ethics: this is a false conflict, because there is no real confrontation, since the two terms are not on the same plane. There is no ethics of information.

What defines otherness is not that the two terms are not identifiable, but that they are not opposable. Otherness is of the order of the incomparable. It is not exchangeable in terms of a general equivalence; it is not negotiable; and yet it circulates in the mode of complicity and the dual relation, both in seduction and in war.

It is not even opposed to identity: it plays with it, just as illusion is not opposed to the real, but plays with it, and as the simulacrum is not opposed to truth, but plays with truth – doing so, therefore, beyond true and false, beyond difference – and just as the feminine is not opposed to the masculine, but plays with the masculine, somewhere beyond sexual difference. The two terms do not correlate: the second always plays with the first. The latter is always a more subtle reality which enwraps the former in the sign of its disappearance. The whole effort will be to reduce this antagonistic principle, this incompatibility, to a mere difference, to a well-tempered play of opposition, to a negotiation of identity and difference in place of the stolen otherness.

All that seeks to be singular and incomparable, and does not enter into the play of difference, must be exterminated. Either physically or by integration into the differential game where all singularities vanish into the universal field. So it is with primitive cultures, for example: their myths have become comparable under the aegis of structural analysis. Their signs have become exchangeable under the umbrella of a universal culture, in exchange for their right to difference. Whether denied by racism or neutralized by differential culturalism, those cultures were faced, at any event, with a final solution. This reconciliation of all antagonistic forms in the name of consensus and conviviality is the worst thing we can do. We must reconcile nothing. We must keep open the otherness of forms, the disparity between terms; we must keep alive the forms of the irreducible.

The 'Laying-Off' of Desire

In facial features, sex, illnesses and death, identity is perpetually changing. This is the body as destiny, which has to be exorcized at all costs – through the appropriation of the body as projection of self, the individual appropriation of desire, of one's appearance, one's image: cosmetic surgery on all fronts. If the body is no longer a site of otherness but of identification, then we have urgently to become reconciled with it, repair it, perfect it, turn it into an ideal object. Everyone treats their bodies the way men treat women in projective identification: they invest them as a fetish, making an autistic cult of them, subjecting them to a quasi-incestuous manipulation. And it is the body's resemblance to its model which becomes a source of eroticism and 'white' seduction – in the sense that it effects a kind of white magic of identity, as opposed to the black magic of otherness.[28]

This is how it is with body-building: you get into your body as you would into a suit of nerve and muscle. The body is not muscular, but muscled. It is the same with the brain and with social relations or exchanges: body-building, brainstorming, word-processing. Madonna is the ideal specimen of this, our muscled Immaculate Conception, our muscular angel who delivers us from the weaknesses of the body (pity the poor shade of Marilyn!).

The sheath of muscles is the equivalent of character armour. In the past, women merely wrapped themselves in their image and their finery – Freud speaks of those people who live with a kind of inner mirror, in a fleshly, happy self-reference. That narcissistic ideal is past and gone; body-building has wiped it out and replaced it with a gymnastic Ego-Ideal – cold, hard, stressed, artificial self-reference. The construction of a double, of a physical and mental identity shell. Thus, in 'body simulation', where you can animate your body remotely at any moment, the phantasy of being present in more than one body becomes an operational reality. An extension of the human being. And not a metaphorical or poetic extension, as in Pessoa's heteronyms, but quite simply a technical one.[29]

The contemporary individual is never without his clones – reincarnation of the old fatality of incest, of the infernal cycle of identity which, at least in the fable, still had an air of tragic destiny to it but which, for us, is now no longer anything but the code of the automatic disappearance of the individual. We can't exactly even speak of individuals any longer. Individuation was part of the golden age of a subject–object dynamics. Since he has become truly indivisible, and has thus achieved his perfect – that is to say, delirious, self-referential – form, we cannot speak of the individual any longer, but only of the Selfsame and the hypostasis of the Selfsame. As is illustrated by the absolute, intransitive difference which marks the final point of that self-reference: 'my', 'your', 'his or her' difference. The pure and simple appropriation of difference. Previously, it was at least the other who was taken to be different. Metastases of identity: all the particles disperse into individual histories. To each his cocktail, his own life story, all equivalent in their simultaneously differential and insignificant character. Each one defended by such a scrambling system that his voice, speech and face will soon be unrecognizable to the others, except to those who have a personal decoder – including when making love: the body will materialize only for those who have the key to the decoder. Soon we shall all be decoding machines. Since every spontaneous relationship, every natural movement of desire, is laid off [*en chômage technique*], then the technical ritual will have to substitute for this 'technically' unemployed desire.

Madonna Deconnection:[30] Madonna is 'desperately' fighting in a world where there is no response – the world of sexual indifference. Hence the urgent need for hypersexual sex, the signs of which are exacerbated precisely because they are no longer addressed to anyone. This is why she is condemned successively and simultaneously to take on all the roles and all the versions of sex (rather than the perversions), because for her there is no longer any sexual otherness, something which brings sex into play beyond sexual difference, and not just by parodying it wildly, but always from within. She is, in fact, fighting against her own sex; she is fighting against her own body. For want of some other who would deliver her from herself, she is unrelentingly forced to provide her own sexual enticement, to build up for herself a panoply of accessories – in the event a sadistic panoply, from which she tries to wrench herself away. Harassment of the body by sex, harassment of sex by signs.

It is said that she lacks nothing (this might be said of women in general). There are, however, different ways of lacking nothing. She lacks nothing by virtue of the artefacts and technology with which she surrounds herself, in the manner of a woman producing and reproducing herself – herself and her desire – in a cycle or closed circuit. She lacks precisely that nothing (the form of the other?) which would undress her and deliver her of all this panoply. Madonna is desperately seeking a body able to generate illusion, a naked body costumed by its own appearance. She would like to be naked, but she never manages it. She is perpetually harnessed, if not by leather and metal, then by the obscene desire to be naked, by the artificial mannerism of exhibition. But this produces total inhibition and, for the spectator, radical frigidity. So, paradoxically, she ends up personifying the frenetic frigidity of our age.

She can play all the roles. But is this because she enjoys a solid identity, a fantastic power of identification, or because she has none at all? Surely because she has none. But the trick is to know – as she does – how to exploit this fantastic absence of identity.

We know people who, for want of being able to communicate, are victims of profuse otherness (as we speak of profuse sweating). They play all the roles at once, their own and the other person's; they both give and return, ask the questions and supply the answers. They embrace the other's presence so fully that they no longer know the limits of their own. The other is merely a transitional object. The secondary gain from the loss of the other is an ability to transform oneself into anyone at all – through role-playing, virtual and computer games, through that new spectrality Marc Guillaume speaks of, with the age of Virtual Reality still to come, when we shall don otherness like a data suit.

This whole movement of construction of an artificial double of the body and desire ends in the pornographic, the culmination of a henceforth desireless hyper-body, of a now indifferent and useless sexual function. But a function which works all the better in sex-processing, like text in word-processing, art in art-processing, war in war-processing, and so on. It is in this transparency, this charnel house of signs of the body disincarnate, that pornographic images move (it is, indeed, transparency itself that is pornographic, not the lascivious obscenity of the body): everything is presented to the gaze there with a kind of objective irony. Transgression, prohibitions, phantasies, censorship – everything is presented as phallic 'quotation'. It is the minimal illusion of sex: become cool, ironic and promotional, porn has definitely not gained anything in pagan innocence, but it has gained something in media insolence.

It is the pure form of sex which can no longer be said to be encumbered by the mystery of sexual difference, nor the figures of otherness attaching to it. The signs of masculine and feminine no longer function there as such (as they do in erotic art) but as something purely sexual, dispelling all ambiguity: sexual difference is suddenly realized in its objective, anatomical, technical form as a surgical mark. The pornographic is thus the model of a society where sexual difference and the difference between reality and the image both disappear at the same time, and all registers become eroticized as they fall into non-distinction and the confusion of genres. Thus, if it was possible for la Cicciolina to be elected a member of the Italian Parliament, this is because the political and the sexual, having become transpolitical and transsexual, meet in the same ironic indifference. This previously unthinkable achievement is the mark of the profound travestying of our culture. The state of prostitution is quite simply that of the total substitution of terms, sexes and categories one for another.

In reality there no longer is any identifiable pornography, because the essence of the pornographic has passed into things, into images, into all the techniques of the visual and the virtual – all of which, in a way, deliver us from that collective phantasmagoria. We are doubtless merely play-acting obscenity, play-acting sexuality, as other societies play-act ideology, as Italian society, for example (though it is not the only one), play-acts power. Thus, in advertising, it is merely the comedy of the bared female body that is being played out. Hence the error of feminist recriminations: if this perpetual striptease and sexual blackmail were real, that would be unacceptable. Not morally unacceptable, but unacceptable because we would be exposed to pure obscenity, that is to say, the naked truth, the mad pretension of things to express their truth (this is the nauseous secret of TV 'reality shows'). Fortunately, we have not reached that point. The hyperreality of everything in our culture and the High Definition which underlines its obscenity are too glaring to be true. And so they protect us by their very excess. As for art, it is too superficial to be truly worthless. There must be some mystery to it. There must surely be some meaning to such a riot of sex and signs, but we can't see what it is. Perhaps this worthlessness, this meaninglessness, take on a sense when they are viewed from another world, from another angle, like objects in anamorphosis? In the unreality of porn, in the insignificance of images, in all the figures of simulation, there is an allegory running beneath the surface, an enigma lurking in it all like a negative image – who knows? If everything becomes too obvious to be true, then there's still a chance for illusion. What lurks behind this moronic world? Another form of intelligence or a definitive lobotomy?

The dictatorship of images is, at any rate, an ironic dictatorship. Take Jeff Koons and la Cicciolina, and their erotic, allegorical, infantile, incestuous machine – at Venice, they came together to mime their real coupling in front of the depiction of that coupling. Autoerotic confusion, new aphrodisiac mysticism, no more and no less carnal or provocative than the fluorescent or geometric erectility of Gilbert and George.

Obscenity may be sublime or grotesque, if it shatters the innocence of a natural world. But what can porn do in a world pornographied in advance? What can art do in a world simulated and travestied in advance? Except bring an added ironic value to appearances? Except tip a last paradoxical wink – of sex laughing at itself in its most exact and hence most monstrous form, laughing at its own disappearance beneath its most artificial form?

What solution is there? There is no answer to this collective syndrome of a whole culture, this fascination, this mad whirl of denial of otherness, of all strangeness, all negativity, this repudiation of evil and reconciliation around the selfsame and its multiple figures: incest, autism, twinship, cloning. We can only remember that seduction resides in the safeguarding of alienness, in non-reconciliation. One should not be reconciled with one's body, nor with oneself, one should not be reconciled with the other, one should not be reconciled with nature, one should not reconcile male and female, nor good and evil. Therein lies the secret of a strange attraction.

The New Victim Order

Just as the whole movement of technical construction of the body and desire ends in the pornographic, so the whole movement of an indifferent society ends in victimhood and hatred.

Doomed to our own image, our own identity, our own 'look', and having become our own object of care, desire and suffering, we have grown indifferent to everything else. And secretly desperate at that indifference, and envious of every form of passion, originality or destiny. Any passion whatever is an affront to the general indifference. Anyone who, by his passion, unmasks how indifferent, pusillanimous or half-hearted you are, who, by the force of his presence or his suffering, unmasks how little reality you have, must be exterminated. There you have the other resuscitated, the enemy at last re-embodied, to be subjugated or destroyed.

Such are the incalculable effects of that negative passion of indifference, that hysterical and speculative resurrection of the other.

Racism, for example. Logically, it should have declined with the advance of Enlightenment and democracy. Yet the more hybrid our cultures become, and the more the theoretical and genetic bases of racism crumble away, the stronger it grows. But this is because we are dealing here with a mental object, an artificial construct, based on an erosion of the singularity of cultures and entry into the fetishistic system of difference. So long as there is otherness, strangeness and the (possibly violent) dual relation – as we see in anthropological accounts up to the eighteenth century and into the colonial phase – there is no racism properly so-called. Once that 'natural' relation is lost, we enter into a phobic relationship with an artificial other, idealized by hatred. And because it is an ideal other, this relationship is an exponential one: nothing can stop it, since the whole trend of our culture is towards a fanatically pursued differential construction, a perpetual extrapolation of the same from the other. Autistic culture by dint of fake altruism.

All forms of sexist, racist, ethnic or cultural discrimination arise out of the same profound disaffection and out of a collective mourning, a mourning for a dead otherness, set against a background of general indifference – a logical product of our marvellous planet-wide conviviality.

The same indifference can give rise to exactly opposite behaviour. Racism is desperately seeking the other in the form of an evil to be combated. The humanitarian seeks the other just as desperately in the form of victims to aid. Idealization plays for better or for worse. The scapegoat is no longer the person you hound, but the one whose lot you lament. But he is still a scapegoat. And it is still the same person.

No pity for Sarajevo[31]

In the programme '*Le couloir pour la parole*' on Arte, with its Strasbourg–Sarajevo link-up, what was striking was the absolute superiority, the exceptional status conferred by misfortune, distress and total disillusionment – that very disillusionment which allowed the people of Sarajevo to treat the 'Europeans' with contempt, or at least with an air of sarcastic freedom which contrasted with the hypocritical remorse and contrition of those who were linked up with them. They were not the ones in need of compassion; they had compassion for our wretched destinies.

'I spit on Europe,' said one of them. Nothing offers greater freedom, in fact, or greater sovereignty, than justified contempt – and not even towards the enemy, but towards those basking with their good consciences in the warm sun of solidarity.

And they have seen plenty of these fine friends. Actors have even come from New York to put on *Waiting for Godot* in Sarajevo. Why not *Bouvard et Pécuchet* in Somalia or Afghanistan? Yet the worst part of it isn't the surfeit of cultural fine feeling, but the condescension and the error of judgement. It is they who are the strong ones and we who are weak, going over there looking for the means to make up for our weakness and loss of reality.

Our reality: that is the problem. We have only one, and it has to be saved. 'We have to do something. We can't do nothing.' But doing something solely because you can't not do something has never constituted a principle of action or freedom. Just a form of absolution from one's own impotence and compassion for one's own fate.

The people of Sarajevo do not have to face this question. Where they are, there is an absolute need to do what they do, to do what has to be done. Without illusion as to ends and without compassion towards themselves. That is what being real means, being in the real. And this is not at all the 'objective' reality of their misfortune, that reality which 'ought not to exist' and for which we feel pity, but the reality which exists as it is – the reality of an action and a destiny.

This is why they are alive, and we are the ones who are dead. This is why, in our own eyes, we have first and foremost to save the reality of the war and impose that – compassionate – reality on those who are suffering from it but who, at the very heart of war and distress, do not really believe in it. To judge by their own statements, the Bosnians do not really believe in the distress which surrounds them. In the end, they find the whole unreal situation senseless, unintelligible. It is a hell, but an almost hyper-real hell, made the more hyperreal by media and humanitarian harassment, since that makes the attitude of the whole world towards them all the more incomprehensible. Thus, they live in a kind of spectrality of war – and it is a good thing they do, or they could never bear it.

But we know better than they do what reality is, because we have chosen them to embody it. Or simply because it is what we – and the whole of the West – most lack. We have to go and retrieve a reality for ourselves where the bleeding is. All these 'corridors' we open up to send them our supplies and our 'culture' are, in reality, corridors of distress through which we import their force and the energy of their misfortune. Unequal exchange once again. Whereas they find a kind of additional strength in the thorough stripping-away of the illusions of reality and of our political principles – the strength to survive what has no meaning – we go to convince them of the 'reality' of their suffering – by culturalizing it, of course, by theatricalizing it so that it can serve as a point of reference in the theatre of Western values, one of which is solidarity.

This all exemplifies a situation which has now become general, in which inoffensive and impotent intellectuals exchange their woes for those of the wretched, each supporting the other in a kind of perverse contract – exactly as the political class and civil society exchange their respective woes today, the one serving up its corruption and scandals, the other its artificial convulsions and inertia. Thus we saw Bourdieu and the Abbé Pierre offering themselves up in televisual sacrifice, exchanging between them the pathos-laden language and sociological metalanguage of wretchedness. And so, also, our whole society is embarking on the path of commiseration in the literal sense, under cover of ecumenical pathos. It is almost as though, in a moment of intense repentance among intellectuals and politicians, related to the panic-stricken state of history and the twilight of values, we had to replenish the stocks of values, the referential reserves, by appealing to that lowest common denominator that is human misery, as though we had to restock the hunting grounds with artificial game. A victim society. I suppose all it is doing is expressing its own disappointment and remorse at the impossibility of perpetrating violence upon itself.

The New Intellectual Order everywhere follows the paths opened up by the New World Order. The misfortune, wretchedness and suffering of others have everywhere become the raw material and the primal scene. Victimhood, accompanied by Human Rights as its sole funerary ideology. Those who do not exploit it directly and in their own name do so by proxy. There is no lack of middlemen, who take their financial or symbolic cut in the process. Deficit and misfortune, like the international debt, are traded and sold on in the speculative market – in this case the politico-intellectual market, which is quite the equal of the late, unlamented military–industrial complex. Now, all commiseration is part of the logic of misfortune [*malheur*]. To refer to misfortune, if only to combat it, is to give it a base for its objective reproduction in perpetuity. When fighting anything whatever, we have to start out – fully aware of what we are doing – from evil, never from misfortune.

And the theatre of the transparence of Evil is truly there – at Sarajevo. The repressed canker which corrupts all the rest, the virus of which Europe's paralysis is already the symptom. Europe's furniture is being salvaged at the GATT talks, but it is being burned at Sarajevo. In a sense, this is a good thing. The specious, sham Europe, the Europe botched up in the most hypocritical upheavals, is scuppering itself at Sarajevo. And, in this sense, we might almost see the Serbs as providing the unofficial litmus test, as demystifying that phantom Europe – the Europe of techno-democratic politicians who are as triumphalist in their speeches as they are deliquescent in their actions.

But that is not, in fact, what is really going on here. The real story is that the Serbs, as the vehicles of ethnic cleansing, are at the forefront of the construction of Europe. For it *is* being constructed, the real Europe, the white Europe, a Europe white-washed, integrated and purified, morally as much as economically or ethnically. It is being victoriously constructed at Sarajevo and, in this sense, what is happening there is not an accident at all, but a logical, ascendant phase in the New European Order, that subsidiary of the New World Order, everywhere characterized by white fundamentalism, protectionism, discrimination and control.

It is said that if we just leave things to happen at Sarajevo, we shall be the next to get it. But we already have got it. All the European countries are undergoing ethnic cleansing. This is the real Europe, taking shape in the shadow of the Parliaments, and its spearhead is Serbia. It is no use appealing to some sort of passivity, protesting that we are in some way impotent to do anything about it, since what we have here is a programme that is currently being carried out, a programme in which Bosnia is merely the new frontier. Why do you think Le Pen has largely disappeared from the political stage? Because the substance of his ideas has everywhere filtered into the political class in the form of national opt-outs, cross-party unity, Euro-nationalist instincts and protectionism. No need for Le Pen any more, since he has won, not politically, but virally – in mentalities. Why should this stop at Sarajevo, since what is at stake there is exactly the same? Solidarity will not make a jot of difference to this. It will end, miraculously, the day the extermination has finished, the day the demarcation line of 'white' Europe has been drawn up. It is as though Europe, irrespective of its national distinctions and political differences, had 'taken out a contract' with the Serbs, who have done the dirty deed for it, as the West once took out a contract on Iran with Saddam Hussein. Only, when the hired gun goes too far, he too may have to be bumped off. The operations against Iraq and Somalia were relative failures from the point of view of the New World Order; the Bosnia operation seems set for success so far as the New European Order is concerned.

And the Bosnians know this. They know they are condemned by the international democratic order, not by some hangover from the past or some monstrous excrescence called fascism. They know they are doomed to extermination or banishment or exclusion, like all the heterogeneous and refractory elements the world over – irrevocably so, because whether the kind souls and bad consciences of the West like it or not, that is the inexorable path of progress. The price to pay for Modern Europe will be the eradication of Muslims and Arabs, who are indeed already being eradicated everywhere, except where they remain as immigrant slaves. And the major objection to the bad-conscience offensive, as mobilized in media happenings like the one at Strasbourg, is that by perpetuating the image of the alleged impotence of European policies and the image of a Western conscience racked by its own impotence, it provides a cover for the real operation by lending it the spiritual benefit of the doubt.

The people of Sarajevo shown on Arte certainly looked as if they had no illusions and no hope, but they didn't look like potential martyrs. Far from it. They had their objective misfortune, but the real wretchedness, that of the false apostles and voluntary martyrs, was on the other side. Now, as has very rightly been said, 'no heed will be paid in the hereafter to voluntary martyrdom'.

Victim society as the easiest, most trivial form of otherness. Resurrection of the Other as calamity, as victim, as alibi – and of ourselves as unhappy consciousnesses extracting from this necrological mirror an identity which is itself wretched. We explore the multiple signs of misfortune to prove God by Evil, as we explore the wretchedness of others to prove our existence *a contrario*. The new identity is the victim's identity. Everything is organized around the deprived, frustrated, handicapped subject, and the victim strategy is that of his acknowledgement as such. Every difference is asserted in the victimal mode of recrimination (of the reparation of a crime); others are called on only for purposes of recognition. This is the social sphere as human rights therapy, as surgery for the mending of identities. An effective strategy, this, the strategy of cashing in one's debt, trading on one's losses –

negative blackmail. A defective strategy, one to parallel the strategies of weakness and disbandment. A minimalist, victimalist, humanitarian strategy, characteristic of emotional and promotional societies. Hands off my difference![32]

Rights as universal reference, as underwriting all differences. A hegemony which has little to do with public affairs and the collective institution, but much to do with that kind of contract that indiscriminately sanctions the loss of natural qualities – as, for example, when the right to existence sanctions the loss of the most precious thing obtained without our having a right to it: life. Or when the right to pure air substitutes for asphyxia, the right to freedom for the exercise of freedom, or right itself for desire in the form of the right to desire, and so on. Rights are what mobilize the energies of an enervated social body. Weak value of an existence under guarantee – a formal, insurance-minded, risk-free society.

The assumption of human suffering into the heaven of the media and the mental space of advertising is accompanied by its irruption into political and sociological metadiscourse. This is because politics and sociology are themselves faced with their own destitution. Together, therefore, they have struck a pact with social destitution on the basis of commiseration. Sociologists speak wretchedly, and the wretched set about expressing themselves sociologically. So we move into a situation of the celebration of one's deficit, one's misfortune, one's personal insignificance – with the intellectual and media discourse, by its simultaneously sadistic and sentimental takeover of these matters, sanctioning people's right to their own suffering, their consecration as victims and the loss of their natural defences. The victims themselves do not complain, since they get the benefit of confessing their misery. Foucault argued that a whole culture was at one time engaged in the confession of sex. It has now gone over to the confession of wretchedness.

*   *   *

Atonement, expiation, laundering, prophylaxis, promotion and rehabilitation – it is difficult to put a name to all the various nuances of this general commiseration which is the product of a profound indifference and is accompanied by a fierce strategy of blackmail, of the political takeover of all these negative passions. It is the 'politically correct' in all its effects – an enterprise of laundering and mental prophylaxis, beginning with the prophylactic treatment of language. Black people, the handicapped, the blind and prostitutes become 'people of colour', 'the disabled', 'the visually impaired', and 'sex workers': they have to be laundered like dirty money. Every negative destiny has to be cleaned up by a doctoring even more obscene than what it is trying to hide.

Euphemistic language, the struggle against sexual harassment – all this protective and protectionist masquerade is of the same order as the use of the condom. Its mental use, of course – that is, the prophylactic use of ideas and concepts. Soon we shall think only when we are sheathed in latex. And the data suit of Virtual Reality already slips on like a condom.

Today, the contraceptive sheath is used for seduction. 'He seeks to seduce her, she resists, he brings out his condom, she falls into his arms.' She would, in the past, have been seduced by the erection; now, she is seduced by the protection. A step further, and being HIV positive [*séropositif*] will be seductive in itself ('This product can damage your health' serves almost as an advertising slogan). We have seen on our walls and our buses: 'I'm HIV positive – will you come to the dining hall with me? (say yes!)'; 'I'm a mongol – will you come and play with me?'; *Sero is beautiful*.[33] The direst thing becomes an advertising statement. A new moral order, a new conviviality based on this marvellous legitimacy of difference, even when it is the difference of the negative and the lack of living.

The AIDS obsession doubtless arises from the fact that the exceptional destiny of the sufferers gives them what others cruelly lack today: a strong, impregnable identity, a sacrificial identity –

the privilege of illness, around which, in other cultures, the entire group once gravitated, and which we have abolished almost everywhere today by the enterprise of therapeutic eradication of Evil [*le Mal*]. But in another way, the whole strategy of the prevention of illness merely shifts the problem [*le mal*] from the biological to the social body. All the anti-AIDS campaigns, playing on solidarity and fear – 'Your AIDS interests me' – give rise to an emotional contagion as noxious as the biological. The promotional infectiousness of information is just as obscene and dangerous as that of the virus. If AIDS destroys biological immunities, then the collective theatricalization and brainwashing, the blackmailing into responsibility and mobilization, are playing their part in propagating the epidemic of information and, as a side-effect, in reinforcing the social body's immunodeficiency – a process that is already far advanced – and in promoting that other mental AIDS that is the Aids-athon, the Telethon and other assorted Thanatons – expiation and atonement of the collective bad conscience, pornographic orchestration of national unity.

AIDS itself ends up looking like a side-effect of this demagogic virulence. '*Tu me préserves actif, je te préservatif* ':[34] this scabrous irony, heavy with blackmail, which is also that of Benetton, as it once was of the BNP,[35] in fact conceals a technique of manipulation and dissolution of the social body by the stimulation of the vilest emotions: self-pity and self-disgust. Politicians and advertisers have understood that the key to democratic government – perhaps even the essence of the political? – is to take general stupidity for granted: 'Your idiocy, your resentment, interest us!' Behind which lurks an even more suspect discourse: 'Your rights, your destitution, your freedom, interest us!' Democratic souls have been trained to swallow all the horrors, scandals, bluff, brainwashing and misery, and to launder these themselves. Behind the condescending interest there always lurks the voracious countenance of the vampire.

*　　*　　*

Behind the facelifting of all categories in the name of their difference there always lurks contempt. 'There is nothing to prevent us thinking that a woman or a homosexual will one day become President,' declares an official candidate. As though elevation to the presidency would finally make a woman or a homosexual a full member of the human race! No doubt we must one day give the job to a blind albino mongol with cancer. Already Miss America is deaf and dumb!

In this same way, on the pretext of unconditional respect for life (what could be more politically correct?), we have heard the following humanitarian profession of faith pronounced: no idea in the world is worth killing for (nor, doubtless, worth dying for). No human being deserves to be killed for anything whatsoever. A final acknowledgement of insignificance: both of ideas and of people. This statement, which actually seeks to show the greatest respect for life, attests only to a contempt and an indifference for ideas and for life. Worse than the desire to destroy life is this refusal to risk it – nothing being worth the trouble of being sacrificed. This is truly the worst offence, the worst affront possible. It is the fundamental proposition of nihilism.

Indifference and Hatred

In the past, we had objects to believe in – objects of belief. These have disappeared. But we also had objects not to believe in, which is just as vital a function. Transitional objects, ironic ones, so to speak, objects of our indifference, but objects none the less. Ideologies played this role reasonably well. These, too, have disappeared. And we survive only by a reflex action of collective credulity, which consists not only in absorbing everything put about under the heading of news or information, but in believing in the principle and transcendence of information. While, at the same time, remaining deeply incredulous and resistant to that kind of knee-jerk consensus. We no more believe in information by divine right than serfs ever believed they were serfs by divine right, but we act as though we do. Behind this façade, a gigantic principle of incredulity is growing up, a principle of secret disaffection and the denial of any social bond.

There is a considerable danger of the inertia threshold being crossed, danger of a potential gravitational collapse by an exceeding of the critical mass, thanks to the absorption by the system of all negative elements: crashes, errors, scandals, conflicts – everything is absorbed back into it as though by evaporation. All the wastes and disorders are digested and recycled. Maddening metastability which gives rise to a whole range of violent, virulent, destabilizing abreactions, which are the symptom of that collapse.

All our contemporary passions arise from this: objectless, negative passions, all born of indifference, all built (in the absence of a real object) on a virtual other, and thus doomed to crystallize for preference on any old thing at all.

We are in a social trance: vacant, withdrawn, lacking meaning in our own eyes. Abstracted, irresponsible, enervated. They have left us the optic nerve, but all the others have been disabled. It is in this sense that information has something of dissection about it: it isolates a perceptual circuit, but disconnects the active functions. All that is left is the mental screen of indifference, which matches the technical in-difference of the images.

Like those people walking in the streets of Sarajevo who pass by with just a furtive glance at the body of a woman killed in the shelling, as though at a cat that had been run over. Neither mourning nor compassion. This is exactly the way the whole of Europe passes by the corpse of Bosnia, without any real emotion, except the work of mourning we carry out on ourselves.

Everyone is moving in their own orbit, trapped in their own bubble, like satellites. Strictly speaking, no one has a destiny any more, since there is destiny only where one intersects with others. Now, the trajectories do not intersect (the vague *clinamen* sometimes produced by the sentimental collision of a few atoms cannot be called destiny, nor can the occasional turbulence produced by acceleration). They merely have the same destination. And so, as on interchanges or motorways (and this goes for information superhighways too), people see only those travelling in the same direction. And even then, they see them no more than fish see each other, when they all instantly veer off in the same direction. There is less risk of an accident that way, but the possibility of meeting is non-existent. The other no longer has any but a marginal value.

This is the great syndrome of the social menopause. Allergy to the social, sociality disorders, the end of social ovulation. Allopause: relational disorders. Oneiropause: the end of the ovulation of dreams. Feverishness, anxiety, dizzy spells, default of heirs. Irritation. Everything begins with irritation, the most inoffensive form. A question: 'What gets on your nerves?' In the past, we would have asked what excites you, what outrages you? But we are no longer excited or outraged; things get on our nerves, we are irritated. Irritation is the epidermal fallout of the grand passions, a little burst of reaction to the undesirable, the unbearable daily round. What gets on your nerves? Everything, by definition. Irritation is an allergic form without any definite object, a profuse, diffuse creeping of the flesh, a sidelong sort of affect. Mechanical problems, other people's mannerisms, your own mannerisms, children, objects get on your nerves – their failings, their ruses, their clandestine resistance. Everything which plagues you, everything which has to do with the futile burdening of existence and whose express function it is to irritate you. The French term '*énervement*', which once referred to the severing of the tendons of people who then lay insensible, unable to move, is today synonymous with annoyance and nervous hyperreaction, but the two senses are closely related since this hyperreaction in fact corresponds to a profound disaffection, an annoyed indifference, a devitalization.

Allergy is of the same order: an indefinable form of repulsion, a diffuse abreaction, a repressed hostility, as though the body were attacking itself, producing its annoyance from the inside. It is impatience, or frustrated passion, linked to the suspect otherness of an artificially overcathected world. Every system like our own, which functions by surface impulse, produces this kind of surface repulsion, which is its bodily manifestation. Every society which functions by rejection, by exclusion, causes this kind of inflammation or protective rash – a barrage against the seduction of a world you fear, but also against the crowding-in of a world which disgusts you.

Contrary to the hysteric, who, by making an exhibition of himself, betrays his despair at not being there, allergy testifies to the confusion of being there, and to the excessive presence of the body. Let us not forget that allergy is hypersensitivity to a particular substance. It is an excess of positive reaction. Thus an allergic world is a world of excess, of an oversensitivity to anything whatever – precisely, to others? – but one which turns around in a negative conversion. The same pattern in anorexia: denial of the excess of body, metaphor for the hypertrophy of the system.

All these indifferent passions, or passions born of indifference, all these negative passions, culminate in hatred. A strange expression: 'I've got the hate' [*J'ai la haine*]. No object. It is like 'I'm demonstrating', but for whom, for what? 'I take responsibility' [*J'assume*], but for what? Nothing in particular. One perhaps takes responsibility precisely for the nothing. One demonstrates for or against the nothing – how are we to know? This is the fate of all these intransitive verbs. The graffiti said: 'I exist', 'I live at this particular place'. This was stated with a kind of exultation, yet at the same time it said: 'There is no meaning to my life'. Similarly, 'I've got the hate' says at the same time: 'This hate I have has no object'; 'There's no meaning to it'. Hatred is doubtless something which does indeed outlive any definable object, and feeds on the disappearance of that object. Who are we to take against today? There, precisely, is the object: the absent other of hatred. 'Having' hatred is like a sort of potential of – negative and reactive – energy, but energy all the same. These are, indeed, the only passions we have today: hatred, disgust, allergy, aversion, rejection and disaffection. We no longer know what we want, but we know what we don't want. In its pure expression of rejection, it is a non-negotiable, irremediable passion. Yet there is in it something like an invitation to the absent other to offer himself as an object for that hatred.

The dream of hatred is to give rise to a heartfelt enmity, which is scarcely available at all in our world now, as all conflicts are immediately contained. Over against the hatred born of rivalry and conflict there is a hatred born of accumulated indifference which can suddenly crystallize in an extreme physical outburst. We are not speaking of class hatred now, which, paradoxically, remained a bourgeois passion. That had a target, and was the driving force behind historical action. This hatred is externalized only in episodes of 'acting-out'. It does not give rise to historical violence, but to a virulence born of disaffection with politics and history. In this sense, it is the characteristic passion not of the end of history but of a history without end, a history which is a dead-end, since there has been no resolution of all the problems it posed. It is possible that beyond the end, in those reaches where things turn around, there is room for an indeterminate passion, where what remains of energy also turns around, like time, into a negative passion.

A negative passion cannot become universal. You cannot imagine a federation of hatreds. You might almost wish to see such a scenario come about. But the worst situation doesn't always materialize. The fact remains that from this point on there is something which is completely beyond social regulation. If this is not the end of History, it is certainly the end of the social. We are no longer in anomie, but in anomaly. Anomaly is what escapes not only the law but the rule. What is outside the game, 'offside', no longer in a position to play. The outlaw space bred violence; this offside space breeds virulence. But as to what exactly is being bred in anomaly, we have no notion. When a system becomes universal (the media, networks, the financial markets, human rights), it automatically becomes anomalous and secretes virulences of all kinds: financial crashes, AIDS, computer viruses, deregulation, disinformation. Hatred itself is a virus of this kind.

Take Paulin, the man from Guadeloupe who went around murdering old ladies a few years ago. A monstrous individual, but cool, and with no apparent hatred in him. He had no identity, and was of indeterminate sex and mixed race. He committed his murders without violence or bloodshed. And he recounted them with an odd detachment. Being indifferent to himself, he was eliminating people who were themselves indifferent. But we can assume that behind all this there was a deep fund of radical hatred. Doubtless Paulin 'had the hate', but he was too classy, too educated, to express it openly.

In the consensual universal order (the New World Order, the New Democratic Order) violent singularities well up, reflecting the extent of the inadmissibility of that order. The principle of negotiation and reconciliation at any price is a principle implying a final solution, which sometimes leads to 'the' final solution. We do not need psychoanalysis to tell us that man is an ambiguous, untameable animal, and that it is senseless to attempt to extirpate evil from him in order to turn him into a rational being. Yet it is upon this absurdity that all our progressive ideologies are based.

In the process, a residue is left over which is not dealt with because it cannot be, and naturally this becomes transformed into hatred. In this sense, hatred, a viral passion, is also a vital passion. Against the perfection of the system, hatred is a last vital reaction.

It is the same sentiment which, in all non-Western peoples, fuels that deep, visceral denial of what we represent and what we are. As though those peoples also 'had the hate'. We can lavish on them all the universal charity we are capable of, but there is about them a kind of otherness which will not be understood, a kind of incompatibility which will not be bargained away. The gulf between our culture of the universal and what remains of singularities is growing firmer and deeper. Their *ressentiment* may be impotent, but from the depths of their virtual extermination a passion for revenge is infiltrating and dislocating the Western world, just as the ghost of the excluded is beginning to haunt our conventional societies.

The Revenge of the Mirror People

Here begins the great revenge of otherness, of all the forms which, subtly or violently deprived of their singularity, henceforth pose an insoluble problem for the social order, and also for the political and biological orders.

In those days the world of mirrors and the world of men were not, as they are now, cut off from each other. They were, besides, quite different; neither beings nor colours nor shapes were the same. Both kingdoms, the specular and the human, lived in harmony; you could come and go through mirrors. One night the mirror people invaded the earth. Their power was great, but at the end of bloody warfare the magic arts of the Yellow Emperor prevailed. He repulsed the invaders, imprisoned them in their mirrors, and forced on them the task of repeating, as though in a kind of dream, all the actions of men. He stripped them of their power and of their forms, and reduced them to mere slavish reflections. Nonetheless, a day will come when the magic spell will be shaken off . . . shapes will begin to stir. Little by little they will differ from us; little by little they will not imitate us. They will break through the barriers of glass or metal and this time will not be defeated.

J.L. Borges[36]

Such is the allegory of otherness vanquished and condemned to the servile fate of resemblance. Our image in the mirror is not innocent, then. Behind every reflection, every resemblance, every representation, a defeated enemy lies concealed. The Other vanquished, and condemned merely to be the Same. This casts a singular light on the problem of representation and of all those mirrors which reflect us 'spontaneously' with an objective indulgence. None of that is true, and every representation is a servile image, the ghost of a once sovereign being whose singularity has been obliterated. But a being which will one day rebel, and then our whole system of representation and values is destined to perish in that revolt. This slavery of the same, the slavery of resemblance, will one day be smashed by the violent resurgence of otherness. We dreamed of passing through the looking-glass, but it is the mirror peoples themselves who will burst in upon our world. And 'this time will not be defeated'.

What will come of this victory? No one knows. A new existence of two equally sovereign peoples, perfectly alien to one another, but in perfect collusion? Something other, at least, than this subjection and this negative fatality.

So, everywhere, objects, children, the dead, images, women, everything which serves to provide a passive reflection in a world based on identity, is ready to go on to the counter-offensive. Already they resemble us less and less . . .

I'll not be your mirror![37]

To sum up, we find ourselves faced with a dual project: a bid to complete the world, to achieve an integral reality – and a bid to continue the Nothing (of which the book is a part). Both are doomed to fail. But, whereas the failure of an attempt at completion is, necessarily, negative, the failure of an attempt at annihilation is, necessarily, vital and positive. It is for this reason that thought, which knows it will fail in any case, is duty-bound to set itself criminal objectives. An undertaking directed towards positive objectives cannot allow itself to fail. One which pursues criminal objectives is duty-bound to fail. Such is the well-tempered application of the principle of evil.

If the system fails to be everything, nothing will remain of it. If thought fails to be nothing, something will remain of it.

TRANSLATOR'S NOTES

1. As ever in my translation of this term, I have retained 'transparence' to mark a distinction from 'transparency' in its everyday sense. This solution was arrived at after discussion with the author.
2. Henri Michaux (1899–1984), Belgian-born French poet and painter.
3. The French verb '*altérer*' has the sense of making something other than its (perfect?) self and thus of distorting, impairing or even falsifying it. In parts of this chapter and in other parts of this book, the word has, therefore, been translated by an equivalent English term, such as 'impair'. However, since – particularly in the early chapters of this work – Baudrillard's argument depends both on (French) meaning and (shared French and English) etymology, I have found it necessary to invent an English verbal form 'alter-ed' and a related noun 'alter-ation', which I must ask the reader to understand as involving a *negative* alteration, a change *for the worse*. I have tried to use this as sparingly as possible, and wherever '*altérer*' seems to me to be employed to describe a relatively 'neutral' change, I have used the ordinary English 'alter'.
4. There is a play here on the French verb '*se dérober*', which normally means 'to hide or conceal itself'.
5. Baudrillard's expression '*la constellation du secret*' refers to a passage in Martin Heidegger's 'The Question Concerning

Technology', which William Lovitt renders as 'the constellation, the stellar course of the mystery' (*The Question Concerning Technology and other Essays*, Harper Colophon Books, Harper & Row, New York 1977, p. 33). For this reason, the French word 'secret' has been treated here as equivalent to the German *Geheimnis* and has, at times, been translated as 'mystery' in other related contexts.

6. By Kawabata Yasunari.

7. The French expression here, '*rester sur sa fin*', is a play on the expression '*rester sur sa faim*', which literally means to remain hungry, but is used metaphorically in the sense of being left 'up in the air'.

8. There are, to my knowledge, three films which bear this title, the first dating from 1913. Internal evidence from other texts suggests that the author is probably referring either to Henrik Galeen's silent version of 1926 or to the German film of 1936 made by the Chicago-born director Arthur Robison.

9. Stephen Jay Gould, *The Flamingo's Smile: Reflections in Natural History*, Penguin, Harmondsworth 1991, p. 108 (first published 1985).

10. Those inclined to search for this quotation in Ecclesiastes would be better advised to consult Baudrillard's *Fragments. Cool Memories III*, Éditions Galilée, Paris 1995.

11. In Arthur C. Clarke, *Of Time and Stars*, Roc (an imprint of Penguin Books) in association with Victor Gollancz, London 1992, pp. 15–23.

12. '*Reality show*' is the term that has been imported into French to describe those TV programmes which deal mainly in personal confessions and 'real-life' stories, the most prominent of which has been Mireille Dumas's *Bas les Masques* on France 2.

13. Peter Schlemihl is the eponymous hero of *Peter Schlemihls wundersame Geschichte* (1814) by the French-born poet, translator, botanist and philologist Adelbert von Chamisso (1781–1838). Schlemihl's 'remarkable story' comes about in large part as a result of selling his shadow to the devil.

14. The phrase 'total achievement' is in English in the original.
15. The term 'think-operator' is in English in the original.
16. This translation of the French term 'dénégation' – which I do not usually favour, since it is at variance with normal English usage – has been employed here because Baudrillard is playing upon an affinity (and also, of course, an antithesis) between this term and the newly coined 'dé-négation' in the previous sentence. 'Dénégation' is frequently used by French theorists to translate the Freudian '*Verleugnung*', when it is perhaps best rendered as 'denial' or 'disavowal'. This latter is, however, also a de-negation of sorts, since in its earliest Freudian usage it is the denial *of an absence* (the absence of a penis in the girl).
17. The French comic magazine *Hara Kiri* has for many years employed this expression (literally: 'stupid and nasty') as its device.
18. Characters in Jarry's Ubu plays, rendered into English as 'Palcontents' in Cyril Connolly and Simon Watson Taylor's 1968 translation, 'Ubu Rex', *The Ubu Plays*, Methuen, London 1968.
19. Epigraph in English in the original.
20. Warhol, *From A to B and Back Again: The Philosophy of Andy Warhol*, Pan, London 1976, pp. 17–18.
21. The 'Perfect' were those Cathars who had been 'consoled', i.e. had received the gift of the Paraclete.
22. The two passages in quotation marks, and the chapter title, are in English in the original.
23. *Chuang Tzu*, trans. Herbert A. Giles, Unwin, London 1980, p. 171.
24. Jorge Luis Borges, 'The Babylon Lottery', trans. Anthony Kerrigan, in *Fictions*, John Calder, London 1965, pp. 59–65.
25. A reference to the famous section of Sade's *La philosophie dans le boudoir* entitled '*Français, encore un effort si vous voulez être républicains*'.

26. This phrase echoes the socialist dictum that the workers themselves will bring about their own emancipation.
27. The references here are to Dino Buzzati's *Il crollo della Baliverna* and to Jorge Luis Borges, 'Of Exactitude in Science', in *A Universal History of Infamy*, Allen Lane, London 1973, p. 141.
28. The French here, '*séduction blanche*', implies that the seduction is, like *un mariage blanc*, unconsummated.
29. Fernando Pessoa (1888–1935), Portuguese modernist poet.
30. The words 'Madonna Deconnection' are in English (?) in the original.
31. This text first appeared in *Libération*, 6 January 1994. The television programme referred to was a special broadcast of Arte's political weekly, *Transit*, billed in fact as 'Sarajevo–Strasbourg, un corridor pour la parole' and shown live on Sunday 19 December 1993.
32. The French here, '*Touche pas à ma différence*', is presumably an allusion to the anti-racist slogan '*Touche pas à mon pote!*' (Hands off my pal!).
33. Italicized text in English in the original.
34. Literally: 'You keep me active, I condom you'.
35. The Banque Nationale de Paris was responsible for the 'Your money interests us' slogan to which Baudrillard is alluding here.
36. *The Book of Imaginary Beings*, Penguin, Harmondsworth 1974, pp. 67–8.
37. The phrase 'I'll not be your mirror!' is in English in the original.

TRANSLATIONS FROM VERSO

T.W. Adorno
In Search of Wagner
Translated by Rodney Livingstone

T.W. Adorno
Minima Moralia
Translated by E.F.N. Jephcott

T.W. Adorno
Quasi una Fantasia
Translated by Rodney Livingstone

Giorgio Agamben
Infancy and History
Translated by Liz Heron

Louis Althusser
For Marx
Translated by Ben Brewster

Louis Althusser
Philosophy and the Spontaneous Philosophy of the Scientists
Translated by Ben Brewster et al.

Marc Augé
Non-Places
Translated by John Howe

Etienne Balibar
The Philosophy of Marx
Translated by Chris Turner

Georges Bataille
The Absence of Myth: Writings on Surrealism
Translated by Michael Richardson

Jean Baudrillard
America
Translated by Chris Turner

Jean Baudrillard
Cool Memories
Translated by Chris Turner

Jean Baudrillard
The System of Objects
Translated by James Benedict

Jean Baudrillard
The Transparency of Evil
Translated by James Benedict

Walter Benjamin
Charles Baudelaire
Translated by Harry Zohn

Walter Benjamin
One-Way Street
Translated by Edmund Jephcott and Kingsley Shorter

Walter Benjamin
Understanding Brecht
Translated by Anna Bostock

Walter Benjamin
The Origins of German Tragic Drama
Translated by John Osborne

Norberto Bobbio
Liberalism and Democracy
Translated by Martin Ryle and Kate Soper

Momme Brodersen
Walter Benjamin
Translated by Malcolm Green

Guy Debord
Comments on the Society of the Spectacle
Translated by Malcolm Imrie

Guy Debord
Panegyric
Translated by James Brook

Régis Debray
Media Manifestos
Translated by Eric Rauth

Midas Dekkers
Dearest Pet
Translated by Paul Vincent

Gilles Deleuze and Félix Guattari
What Is Philosophy?
Translated by Graham Burchell and Hugh Tomlinson

Mario Perniola
Enigmas
Translated by Christopher Woodall

José Pierre, ed.
Investigating Sex: Surrealist Discussions 1928–32
Translated by Malcolm Imrie

Jacques Rancière
On the Shores of Politics
Translated by Liz Heron

Rudi Visker
Michel Foucault
Translated by Chris Turner